I am the boss of my sexlife

Chantal Ross

This book is dedicated to all women and girls who have suffered indignities, physical and mental abuse as well as sexual frustration from men, in the name of love.

Contents

Acknowledgements

I thank my amazing children D. and M., who still love me even after finding out mummy is an actual woman.

I thank Muniqui M. and Bill R., two good male friends who love me enough to explain men's point of view without suggesting I should change who I am. That's what friends do.

I am grateful to all the funny, warm and sexy men I dallied with and learned from. Even the useless ones have taught me something. As to the ones I have truly loved... You know who you are.

Thank you to all the girls and women who opened their hearts to me, often in tears, when we tried to make sense of our interactions with gentlemen or thugs.

Special thanks to Arianne T., whose logical, Cartesian mind and her insight into me were precious in editing my adventures in a more ordered manner than I had at first.

Gratitude fills my heart for my cat, which patiently purred entire nights watching me write and always gave me her opinion on my male visitors thanks to her "jerk-radar".

1. The point of this book is...

Every single experience I'm sharing with you has actually happened to me, some recently, some a few months or a few years ago. The bad as well as the ridiculous or the sublime: every single word is true.

Names and places have been changed in order to respect everyone's privacy but the actual facts are real.

When it went well it was fabulous, but when it went less well it was awful, painful and humiliating, still I'm sharing this with you because the point of this book is not to glorify myself but to show you that *You*, ladies, no longer have to suffer in order to have great sex. It can be done harmoniously and without drama.

Each and every man I'm telling you about has existed; some of them are still relevant in my life. Some are definitely worth knowing, some I wish I had never met, some I miss and some are a big joke. Yet I have no regrets, for each and everyman I dated has taught me something valuable.

Why am I exposing myself?

I want to show you my sisters that there is a way out of the patriarchal pre-established "mother or whore" stereotype.

You can be as sexually active as a man while still being a responsible worker, a loving mother, a caring friend, a tax payer, a voter, a Church goer and a decent member of society.

You can have it all if you want to.

I am strong without being brutal, gentle without being weak, loving without being naive. Those are choices that I have made.

Leading such a life requires a little discipline, a sense of humour and some faith. Being a party animal is perfectly acceptable when you still show up for work or meetings on time with a clear head and in full professional mode.

Bed hopping from men to men without your family having any clue as to your nightly activities is, in my opinion, much more productive than constantly looking for "mister right", or to impose some kind of stepfather on your children. Let's not even speak of the possible danger of marrying a paedophile who pretends he wants you in order to have power over your young children.

This was one of my main fears and has greatly influenced my choice to remain single after two trials, just because my husbands were decent men it doesn't mean the third one might have been as well.

Being single is the only way to make sure no one can boss you around after working hours, no one to beat you up or burden you, no one to undermine your authority or undo whatever you got done, no one to take back what they had given you on condition that you would be submissive, no one to interfere in your children's education. And of course there is the big plus of not being accountable to anyone for your actions, unless you wish to be.

Being the boss of your sexlife means you are no longer weak for predators to pretend they are in love with you and leave you confused and humiliated after the deed is done.

Unfortunately, a lot of men will go as far as saying they *"love you"*, that they have *"never felt this way before"* or that *"this is different"*, with the sole purpose of getting laid. And what about women who will endure abuse from their men because they fear *"ending up alone"* or because they think that is the price to pay for having a competent sex partner.

Wouldn't it be more honest to just offer a moment of shared passion with no strings attached?

Why don't men give us the choice of actually having a one night stand or not, instead of pretending they love us so that they can get laid?

When I realized what was going on, I made the conscious decision to behave in a manly way without being predatory. When I like someone I never lie about loving, I'm honest about wanting good sex and leaving afterwards. If men don't like it they can always turn me down, some have because they hated being robbed of the hunting.

Since I'm single, I'm not cheating on a partner that

might get hurt. I do not advocate adultery at all, in fact I was faithful to both my husbands and a couple of boyfriends. I'm proud to say I have never stolen a man from his woman although some women did it to me in the past.

Of course all men are not abusive Cro-Magnons but since so many of them are... safety is in singlehood!

What about love?

It exists and I have twice been the lucky recipient of true love. It is beautiful beyond description and it is the St Grail of sex, the act of love with someone who loves you. Sadly it is mostly short lived and comes at a high price.

What about sex when you are single?

Helloooooooooo!! I'm hereby giving you the ingredients of a magnificent sex life with no price to pay.

In fact, sex is the single woman's best friend, providing you protect yourself physically by using condoms and birth control, and without forgetting to protect yourself emotionally by not falling in love and not getting involved with your lovers.

To those who think only young slim model looking girls can get a fantastic worry free sex life, I will answer the following: sexiness is not a matter of looks or age, it is neither in your bra nor on your face. Sexiness is in your mind. Sexiness is all about confidence. *Sexiness is an attitude.*

Yours truly is 50 years old, plump and only 5"2 (1m57). I don't wear makeup, save red lipstick and I never wear revealing clothes. Yet my nonchalant attitude gets me hot, younger men in bed as much as I want!

Want to know how?

Let's start on my journey to sexual empowerment...

2. Great sex without love

All of us women need to stop playing victims right now. Whatever your age, your origin, credo or social condition, I want you all to know that you can have the joy of sex without the pain of love.

Are you paying attention?

Ok, here it goes.

Sexual attraction is purely physiological. Your body is getting aroused by another body. Your being is sending signals to his, or hers as the case may be.

It can be someone you just met, you shook his hand, you found yourself liking the feel of his skin, its warmth, its muscle tone and when you looked into his eyes you really liked what you saw.

You can be looking across a crowded room at a handsome stranger. He comes over to introduce himself and your mouth goes dry, your pulse is racing and you mumble when he asks you out.

Perhaps you have known this person for a while and feel quite comfortable around him. One day, something is said, something happens that makes you look at him in a new way and you wonder what he would look like on top of you with his hair messed and his body on fire.

You got the picture now? Physical attraction is physical only.

There is no need to pretend you are in love or to tell all your friends you met that great guy. You shouldn't make plans or play hard to get or worry about what he will think of you. He certainly does not.

So somehow you managed to be in bed/in a car/the clubs bathroom/against a door/on the carpet/on your desk, wherever with him (or her). The point is now you are getting sexual with each other. *The secret* is to live the moment to the full. Enjoy this extraordinary gift life is giving you: a moment or night of love making with a cool someone who wants you at the same time you want him.

Just give yourself as much as you want to give and whatever you want to give as far as it is acceptable to you. In my case, I don't do anal sex nor SM stuff, but everything else goes! So do give your body as much as you like at that very moment and take as much from your lover's body too.

Give yourself permission to let go.

Enjoy. Enjoy. Enjoy!

Making love is give, and take, and share, and let's go round again, woohoohoo!

Please, please, please, do not do any thinking during sex. This is the only time when you are truly free, that is the only thing you get to do for yourself. No one can take it away from you. This moment belongs to you and you alone. Put your brain on hold once the condoms are on and the feel good hormones start flowing.

When I was young, stupid and vulnerable, I used to intellectualise my sexual relationships way too much. My man would be shagging my body while my brain was analysing why he had said this and that to me earlier. I would prepare what to tell him afterwards while he had no idea of what was going on. I would wonder if he truly loved me or if he would still have any respect left for me later. Was he comparing me to the girl he dated before me or was he thinking about his new car? How? Why? How? Why?

The result was that I didn't really come and my man would still be on my mind hours after he had left.

How frustrating!

Many women make the same mistake because of the hypocritical sacralisation of sex, designed only to take our power away. Just enjoy the man when he is inside you and don't give him another thought till he is back in your arms. That's all.

And that is the secret of sexual freedom.

In my mid thirties, I got my heart broken for the third time and took a year off sex. Yes, you read this right: I actually took a year off sex. My intention had been to never have sex again in order to never fall in love and get my heart ripped out again. I was in shock and behaved like a spinster.

One night in Zurich, I was having dinner with my friend Leila who was again lamenting that I chucked love out of my life for a man who had rebuilt his. A really cute Irish waiter called Colin (name changed) was serving our food with a friendly smile, big green eyes and pouty lips. Leila's words finally kicked in.

Love is a bitch, I thought, I'm suffering and he has a

new woman! This would never have happened if I had been cold, bitchy and manly. I was going to change my ways, I was going to claim my sexual freedom right now.

I looked at Colin...

"Hey Colin, I haven't had sex since my second husband and I broke up a year ago, do you wanna get together after work and shag? No strings attached. I just wanna feel the joy of sex again."

Poor Colin almost dropped his tray and mumbled:

"I'm your man, meet me back here at eleven thirty and I'll show you the stars."

"Fine, it's a date" I answered and ordered some crème brulée for dessert. Appetite for food was returning to me! How can I describe the shock and disapproval on Leila's face?

"You are not really going to do this, are you?"

"Of course I am, didn't you say I need to *de-spinsterise*?"

"What do you know about that Irish kid? she hissed, and how do you think you will feel afterwards? And anyway we are not going to find out because I'm not letting you do this!"

I patiently justified myself to my friend: "I know what I need to know about that kid, he is sexy, he is willing and I am getting laid tonight after a long dry spell. I don't want to talk or think or feel. I am so tired of living in the memory of my lost love. I am claiming my right to get laid and I am not asking your permission."

Leila was perplex, wondering if my heart break had gone to my head.

As I paid the bill, Colin asked me if I had really meant what I had suggested earlier. Would I have mentioned this if I had not meant it?

I returned at closing time, with Leila on tow, still trying to talk me out of it. Colin arrived and we left.

Back at his place, my Irish waiter was a little nervous, much more than I was and this was MY first experience of loveless sex. He asked me where I came from, did I have any brothers or sisters (*Dude I'm here to release sexual energy, I didn't come here to be questioned*). I undressed and commented on the football world cup which had been won by Italy that very day.

And it happened.

Colin and I had absolutely fabulous sex all night long. To me it was a way to accept that my marriage was really over. Soon it became much more than that, I had so much fun in Colin's arms. I had forgotten what it was like to be kissed, to be held, to feel hands on my body, fingers playing in my then long hair. Feeling a muscular body swinging hips with mine, reminded me how much I was missing out on. Italians motorists would humbly hoot all night and cheer loudly, pleased that they were to have won the world cup again. At some point Colin uttered: "*fucking Italians!*" I giggled and purred... "*a propos fucking...*"

Brilliant! My sense of humour was returning too. I could laugh again, I could make little jokes.

Take the drama out of sex and it makes you feel really alive. That is how I felt the next morning, alive, sexy, born again me!

Next morning at 7 am, I met Leila for breakfast. I was smiling, relaxed and full of life. She was horrified. She asked how anyone could have sex without any emotions to it, outside the concept of a love story. I might as well have used a vibrator or gone to a whore in her opinion. I coolly explained that this was the "new me": feeding on great sexual energy without exposing myself to the cruelty of love again. Shouldn't she be happy for me? When was the last time she had seen me smile? Exactly: too long ago to remember.

The beauty of great sex without the pain of love was going to liberate me. And liberate me it did.

That was one of the best decision I ever took in my life.

3. I cannot sleep with someone I like

Lately I have had a confirmation of something I had suspected for some times. I put men that I like, into 2 categories: the *shag material* and the *friend material*.

Classic Christian education has women thinking that the man in our life has got to be all in one; some kind of all or nothing deal.

The "One" must be the companion, the confidant, the co-bill payer and the genitor of our children. This perfect man must also be able to party with us, play tennis or cards, co-host our dinners, get on with our friends, share our tastes and opinions, be interested in what we have to say, decorate the bathroom, be there for us, be a shoulder to cry on and of course Mr. Right will be the source of our physical pleasure too.

Yeah right!

Sadly, many women actually believe this and it leads to endless delusions and heartaches. My friend Leila once said a husband is really a good girlfriend with a penis.

Why oh why then, do men receive opposite teachings? Boys – most boys anyway – are taught they need one or several women for good sex and fun, lovers, mistresses, one nighters etc. Additionally they need another woman to serve as a companion, raise children, run their household, and perhaps promote their career while putting her own life and career on hold. This woman will be their concubine or wife, with whom they will stop having great sex and fun after a couple of years of marriage but to whom they will stick to the end.

If they can separate women in two categories, so can we.

Let me share with you how brilliantly this system works for me:

The friend material are the men which are smart, opinionated, charming, warm, kind, articulate, have a solid sense of humour and share a few centre of interest with me. Men I could talk to for hours about anything. Those are men I love to befriend, whose advice I seek and value. I'm always proud to have them around my friends and family. I cherish moments with such men friends. It might involve some play flirting, BUT I never have sex with my male friends because I love them too much to jeopardise our friendship.

The shag material are the men who are mindless, meaningless, hot, not always perfect looking but at least very sexy to me. They are funny, charming, smiling, dance well and ooze sensuality through each pore. I never approach any serious topic with such men as I don't want to know their thoughts, credo or histories. Who cares what their favourite actors or books are?

My only condition is that I have to know that those

guys are neither animal/women/children abusers nor racists nor sadists because it is so immoral that it would turn me off permanently.

With my shag material, I'm only prepared to discuss sex topics or neutral subjects. I never talk about my past, my family or my job. It has happened that a shag buddy would question me about personal matter and I would freak out, demanding why they want to know. Usually that is enough for them to understand. If they don't, I can always distract them with kisses.

My shag material men are in my life with the sole purpose of sharing moments of pleasure with me.

That's all.

I don't want to get to know them better: I'm not there to be their girlfriend. In a sex-friendship, you have no expectations from each other and there is no room for misunderstanding. Therefore I never ask them any questions and I expect the same courtesy that I give them.

Of course little accidents can happen. You forget that this is just a sex friendship and you are tempted to linger on too long or even fall in love. When such risky situations take place, it is best to quit immediately before things get out of hand.

I can tell you that every time I have had a moment of weakness with a lover it didn't end well.

Friends can't be messed up with sex and lovers can't be trusted with friendship, I have learned my lesson early in life. These two categories, friends or lovers, need to be separated at all times for me to survive emotionally and sexually.

It works for me, could it work for you too?

4. One girl-two brothers: Chris and Lars in Paris

At some point in my early twenties, I met a charismatic and very sexy bad boy in Paris. Chris and I had a bit of a love/hate relationship for a number of months. He had conveniently forgotten to tell me about a fiancée that he was engaged to and I had omitted to reveal a few things about myself. We were so sexually compatible it almost scared us. We were crazy about each other to the point of insanity. We would fight and break up to then have hot make up sex, tear each other apart only to be uncontrollably drawn back into that toxic connection again. We always knew we were wrong for each other and talked about ways to separate permanently but we just couldn't help ourselves. His family was well off, right wing xenophobes and I was a working class uneducated girl of probably foreign descent. Chris wanted a career in law or in the forces, that meant he should marry someone of his own world like his fiancée was, not a free thinking alley cat like me. We would scream at each other till he would slam the door on his way out. Much later he would get drunk and call in the middle of the night very apologetic, begging for one last chance. I'd say no, never, and he would turn up on my door with teary eyes. One kiss from him and all my anger would melt under his expert caresses. Did I mention Chris was a great lay? The following week I'd try avoiding him, dodging his calls and standing him up, yet still he sought after me. His hungry mouth savoured every inch of me and I just couldn't resist. We felt we were heading for troubles but we couldn't keep our hands off each other. Until one evening...

We had had a heated argument and I went to a new pizzeria by myself to stuff my face and dry my tears. How was I going to pluck Chris out of under my skin?

A gorgeous thing called Lars sat at my table, ordered a Napolitana and started chatting me up. I prefer to eat alone, but that night I was so upset over the Chris situation that I welcomed the distraction. Lars was smart, classy and very articulate. Not to mention confidant and elegant, nothing like my hysterical and over argumentative lover. When Lars made a pass at me, I thought this might be the way to severe myself from my man and I took him back to my place with vengeance on my mind, I just wanted to stop having conversations with Chris in my head. Once we were alone, Lars got crazy, borderline violent. He threw me on the couch and literally tore my clothes off during spectacularly wild shag that matched my angry mood. At some point, my new catch scratched my back till he drew blood; I screamed in pain. Was the dude insane? Lars shut my mouth with a hard kiss every time I complained. I started to worry about my safety when we were done and Lars said he had a confession to make.

There I was, laying on the floor of my living room, next to that explosive stranger, sweaty and out of breath with torn pieces of my jean dress all around me, one ankle boot off and a bloodied back. *Where were my panties?* I wondered. It had been savage and barbarian, quite a lot of fun but I knew I didn't want to repeat it. That Lars was not normal and I wanted him off my carpeted floor and out of my life as soon as possible. Especially since Chris was coming back to my mind. *How was I going to get rid of that man? Get out of my head please? Now*!

Lars got up and pulled his trousers back up.

L-That was terrific! Can I have your number? I want to see you again.

C- I don't think so, that was enjoyable but I do have a boyfriend.

L-I bet he doesn't fuck you like that, though.

C-*That's really none of your business,* I thought. Now I was seriously starting to dislike that guy.

L-You will never have Christopher, you know. His life is already all planned for him and there is no room for you, somebody like you.

My blood froze.

Lars knew! How did he know? Had I been ambushed? How could I have been so stupid and not suspect anything at all?

While I mentally ordered my tears not to burst out, Lars walked towards me and tried to kiss my face. I jumped backwards. Did the creep think I would let him touch me after he had just admitted he had royally screwed me?

L-Christopher and I went to school together and always shared our toys. Now you come along and make him question his life? Not on my watch honey! He is as wrong for you as you are for him. You will not compromise his future. He paused and grinned sexily... but you are just bad enough for me, shall we say tomorrow at eight?

C-You must really be envious of your friend to want a taste of his lover.

L-I'm not envious, I'm just protecting him, that's what big brothers do. That's right... you just slept with your man's brother. He will never forgive you.

I felt nauseated. By now Lars was fully dressed up and had a hand on the door handle.

He turned around.

L-Good luck showering with Christopher with those marks on your back, he knows that's my signature.

I was furious! Why did I have to cheat tonight? What had I done? What had I done?

I decided to sleep on it after a really long shower and I dodged Chris's calls.

The following afternoon, my lover picked me up from work and walked me back to my place. I was silent. Chris was as confused about us as ever, I felt dirty and ashamed. When we went to bed I kept my nightie on to hide my raw back, he thought I was being naughty. We began making out and suddenly I couldn't keep this secret anymore.

C-Lars was here last night, I busted out crying. I'm so sorry. I turned around to show him the proof of my infidelity with his manipulative brother, my sore back full of long scratches.

My boyfriend jumped out of bed with a horrified look on his face.

-What? You slept with my brother? How do you even know Lars? How could you? How could he? How could you? How did he? What!

Embarrassment was choking me, but that was wrong. It is not I who should have felt ashamed; it is Lars for setting me up this way and breaking his brother's heart, betraying his confiding in him. Lars had been despicable, not me!

When my brain got back into gear, I started to tell Chris that he had his brother to blame for this mess. Brother dearest obviously had some issue with him and I had been a collateral damage in their own dirty little war. This was too much for Chris to hear, feeling betrayed as he was by his brother and his girl. Chris shoved me against the wall and made angry love to me, standing up. (I was twenty pounds lighter back then). Was the whole thing turning him on? At some point he pulled my hair back and shouted: "*Salope! Je t'ai dans la peau!*" (*Bitch! you are under my skin*). There is something really hot about a French man saying those words at a strategic time during sex and we came hard together.

I never saw Chris or Lars after that. The whole thing had turned me off. I had no interest in being caught in their twisted power play. Lars did call before I moved out, but I just put the phone down on him. I left Paris to stop fuelling this potential disaster and started a new life abroad.

A few years later I saw Chris on television, he is

now a top police executive. I sometimes see his name in the French papers. He got what he wanted and I'm pleased for him. He had been great in bed... What a shame his evil brother had to mess it up so sordidly.

Ladies, whenever you find yourself involved with two best friends or two brothers, there is only one way to handle it.

Run!

5.   Bad boys VS good boys

In my experience not only are bad boys sexier, regardless of their looks, more confidant because they don't care at all if they get you or not, and they tend to be better in bed because this is the only thing they really have in life. In my opinion it is better to date bad boys rather than good ones because at least you know what to expect.

When a bad boy tries to hurt you, he is usually not very smart about it. You can see him coming miles away and immediately defend yourself, doing some damage control. Bad boys are also quite easy to get over and even easier to replace. A good man stabbing you in the back however, that really hurts.

You had no idea he was going to strike, you thought he was too good and too serious to hit below the belt. But he did. Truth is... good men are really lethal when they hurt you, they are much harder to recover from, and you feel so dumb for not having seen the signs.

That's why I usually stay away from good men.

Each time I date a good man, I am terrified that I won't see it coming and I wonder when he will be going for the kill. Can I allow myself to relax and feel safe around this really nice normal man? After he stabs me in the back as they almost inevitably do, who else will I be able to blame but my stupid trusting self for having ignored the alarm signals that were flying red flags all over?

Looking back on what was said and done, one could almost pinpoint the first signs of danger, the first lies, the first withdrawals of affection, and the first betrayals. Why did we think it was our imagination? Why did we not trust our female instinct? Because that bitch was such a good man he couldn't possibly be manipulative and cruel.

Newsflash ladies: goodies are capable of screwing you far worse than bad boys ever could because goodies have the element of surprise. With bad boys you are always ready to be lied to and hurt in some way. So unless you want boyfriend/husband material: enjoy bad boys (while looking over your shoulder).

6. Rafael, the hot Portuguese waiter from Interlaken

A few weeks ago I attended a conference in the picture pretty city of Interlaken. During lunch break, my colleagues and I went to this posh restaurant to discuss current topics while feasting on delicious Italian food. As I ordered my lemon sauce raviolis I glanced at the waiter, then at my menu, then back at my waiter to notice he had intense brown eyes and a serious amount of Latino bad boy charm while being classy at the same time. He wasn't smiling at me but his eyes were saying it all. I dismissed the thought as wishful thinking on my part. How could that hot young thing desire me at first sight?

When said hot young thing brought my plate, he stared at me silently again, as he was putting my colleagues' plates before them he would pause and give me a sexy stare for a nano second. They all started to eat and talk while I pretended to participate.

Hot young thing was standing behind a counter doing something by the till while still staring at me with those shiny brown eyes. I did what any responsible adult woman would in this situation. I pretended to go to the bathroom to see if he would initiate contact.

He didn't even follow me. Oh man! Did I read him

wrong? Let's go back to my table before embarrassing myself any further, as I open the ladies toilet door, the hot waiter was standing in the frame, staring again but now he was smiling.

"Give me your number and address; I want to make a passionate love with you" he said in a sexy rocky voice. Was that a Spanish accent I was hearing?

"I live in Zurich"

"I hhhave a fasta car"

"Has it occurred to you than one of those men might be my husband and you could be just assuming a lot?"

"I don't think so, I've been watching your body language, you are not with any of them and you keep looking at me. I know you wanta me."

"I *do*" I whispered, giving the gorgeous Spaniard my business card.

Yay! He wants me! He wants me! Now I could relax and get on with lunch and work talks. When we were all leaving, the hot waiter helped me put my coat back on, which I would normally say no to, but I wanted some kind of contact and he took that opportunity to slightly caress the back of my neck.

The conference was over, I sat on my train back home, re-reading the notes I had been taking. My thoughts wandered back to that posh restaurant and the hot Spanish waiter.

Did it really happen? Will he actually call? I wish I

had at least kissed him, given him a taste of things to come... But that guy is like the wind: he appears, makes a strong impression and vanishes again. Nah... He's not going to call, maybe he collects girl's numbers for a kick but doesn't go all the way or maybe I misunderstood or maybe... Ding! A text appeared on my phone screen:

"I will be at your house at 11pm tonight. Rafael"

Yay! It is real, I am getting laid tonight! And with a mysterious Latin lover!

I had been ready for an hour when Rafael rang my bell. Excited as I was, I practically run to the front door before deciding to play cool and slowed down a little. I realised it didn't matter after all, who cared what Rafael would think, I was going to enjoy this mucho macho like there was no tomorrow.

Oh what a night it was going to be!

Rafael walked in without a word, extremely confidant. He pushed me against a wall while kicking the door shut behind him. He kissed me until my head spun, took a step back and starting undressing, throwing his clothes on the floor (*wait a minute...Versace, D & G, Valentino? How does a waiter afford this kind of luxury?*). He sprawled around like a tiger, had the natural elegance of one too. My new conquest opened each door until he found my bedroom... he tilted his head, motioning me to come over. Could he be sexier?

Rafael took in the romantic atmosphere I had created, lots of scented candles, beautiful bedding, Joao Gilberto purring on the stereo...

I guess this was meeting with his approval. Rafael turned around and called out to me: *Vem meu amor.*

A Portuguese! Again! Oh no, I must remember not to have anything to do with Rafael after tonight.

But first, I was going to enjoy the ride.

And what a ride it was... a mix of rough and gentle. Kissing me sensuously one minute and pulling my hair the next. Making sweet love and then riding my body furiously. Soft touching then groping. Sucking my toes slowly but then almost yanking my head off when he came. Rafael was driving me absolutely crazy with the things he was doing to me.

This ocean of madness kept waving over me till 3am.

I was lying on my carpet marvelling at what you can find in a posh restaurant, when Rafael checked his ridiculously expensive designer watch and declared he had to get back to Interlaken to prepare breakfasts. In a flash he was showered and dressed, gave me a hard kiss and jumped in his Porsche.

I watched him drive off noisily. (*Wait... what kind of waiter drives a Porsche? Who cares anyway?*)

This was one of the best one night stands ever, not the very bets, but one of the best. The next morning I sported bruises and could barely sit down, but that had been a phenomenal shag fest.

I never rang Rafael again, neither did he ring me. How awesome that we understood each other while barely talking: two consenting single adults meeting for just one night of fabulous sex and parting on a great memory.

One night stands should always be like this: intense and without follow ups.

7. One night stands save time and energy

Traditionally, a one night stand meant a man asked a girl out, pretending he was very much interested in her and sending signals that this might develop into a relationship of some kind, especially if said girl told the man she did not take sex for a casual matter. The predator always acted and talked in a way that guarantied him plausible deniability later on, in case his prey would complain about his lies that had gotten her to trust him with her body, something she never would have done if she had known this was just a hit and run deal. The next morning, sometimes right after the deed was done, the satisfied guy would just get up, get dressed quickly and walk away from a very confused unsatisfied girl who wondered what she had done wrong. When the predators have the cruelty to pretend asking for a number, the illusion goes on for another couple of days when the victim wonders why he is not calling and should she start making plans without him. After this, the victim finally understands the bleak truth.

She has been used for a one night stand, used, manipulated, lied to, conned, taken for a ride, humiliated.

How many girls and women have suffered from this cruel game? Billions? Trillions? Sadly this still happens in our day and age.

Now, we can reverse this ugly tradition and play men's games to our advantage. That's what I do and it not only gives me total control of my sexuality and my emotions, it empowers me to a point I never knew existed. No more pinning for a special man, no more sitting by the phone or checking my mobile constantly for his hypothetical calls, no more sadness, no more victimisation. No more hesitating dating someone else because I don't know if I'm still with that other one or not. No more.

Have you any idea how good it feels to be so liberated? You can have this power too, if you appoint yourself boss of your own sexlife.

Let's look into a few one night stands I had. You will notice that I have complete control of the situation and the guy has no power over me at all, when he tries to be macho, hurtful, dominant, or all of the above.

Dylan, a really cute Albanian who makes a living sweeping the streets of Zurich. So what if it is not a glamorous job? At least it is an honest job. I met Dylan while queuing up for a Chinese take away in town. He made a few jokes in Italian with his friends and I couldn't help laughing, when he realised I understood him, he made me laugh even harder and started hitting on me in a very cheeky way. I loved his smile and his sense of humour. Beside the fact that Dylan was not at all my type of man, (he was short, skinny and very pale) I tried to visualise what he would look like in the throw of passion and I liked what I saw. Dylan asked me out for coffee, I answered "No thanks, I don't drink coffee, would you like to have sex with me instead?"

A very stunned Dylan blushed and asked what I meant. I started purring in his ear:

"What I mean is: you and I having a hot one night stand tonight back at my place, having a great time and leaving it at that. Want my address?"

Dylan took my business card and hid it in his pocket before anyone noticed asking if he should bring condoms. I thought it cute that he rang twice to ask if I were by myself.

"Of course I'm alone, I said a one night stand not a roman orgy," I giggled.

At first he was nervous, slowly realising that it was I who had chosen him and not the other way around. As I always do, I had immediately told my new one night stand how old I was, he turned out Dylan was in fact nineteen years younger than myself and looking forward to experimenting sex with an older woman. Sex with Dylan was gentle, nice and cuddly. Too bad he was not circumcised, there was a little too much skin for my taste, but he did sport a huge gothic tattoo. Who knew? When we were done, basquing in post sex bliss, he had the audacity to ask the dreaded question...:

"How many guys have been in your bed before me?" Why would he spoil a nice moment with such a heinous question? Because I liked Dylan I diplomatically answered:

"I have been in love three times, the rest doesn't matter."

We parted on a kiss and I didn't see Dylan anymore for about a month. When I ran into him at Starbucks he was very sweet until he said his wife was pregnant. Did he really not notice he had a wife before he had a roll in the hay with me? I remained ladylike and congratulated him before leaving the coffee shop. I felt his hand on my neck...

"It doesn't matter does it? After all it was only a one night stand, you must have known I was married, it is ok, right?"

How would I have known this? Dylan wore no wedding rings and had found it convenient to have a selective amnesia that night. How was I to know I was doing something I totally disapprove of? No it was not ok! Did the silly boy want absolution from me? I didn't make any comments.

"Have a nice day" I said.

He went on and on, "I got to be a good boy now, you know, with another baby on the way and all." What a hypocrite, Dylan, I get your point, it's ok.

"However, he insisted, I need to tell you that I had a dream about you. "

"Have you really?" I asked politely.

"In my dream, you and I were making out in your bed when that cute waitress came along and we ended up doing it together, the three of us... you know... do you think we could talk to her and make this come true?"

What is it with men and threesome?

"Look Dylan, I sighed impatiently, the best thing

about fantasies is just that, they remain in fantasy land, if you try to do it for real you will be disappointed."

"So not true, he squealed, it was my dream to sleep with an older woman and it was great!"

"That's because that was with me, I flirted, but I don't do threesomes and you got to behave yourself for your family."

"What a shame", he whispered before walking away. The translation of this was very clear: "If you want to sleep with me again, you will do as I want, or else there will be no more of this."

Lucky me, having sex with Dylan straight away meant I had a look into his real personality and found out quickly that he was a little creep. Wanting only a one night stand with Dylan meant I did not fear not having him again and therefore did not have to give in to his emotional blackmail.

I love going to the movies on day time, there is practically no one there, no disturbing coughs, no kicks in the back of my sit, no noise. I love it. Jakob was a gorgeous usher who wondered why I was even there when the house was empty; he seemed to understand my reasons. During the break, Jakob sat with me and we had a chat. That would have been impossible had the house been full. I learned that he was from Slovakia on a linguistic course, must be why we spoke in English and not in German. I offered Jakob to come see me the following day for some fun with no strings attached. He came; we had a pleasant conversation and a pleasant romp on the couch.

Later on Jakob morphed into a self absorbed jerk. Talking endlessly about his complicated cursus and the great professional future he had ahead of him. Fine, I thought, you can leave now so that I can have a shower and read a book. When he was done advertising himself Jakob asked a really, really stupid question. "So, how does it feel to sleep with a young man?"

I refrained from laughing and replied: "Feels no different from all the young men I sleep with."

There!

"You mean you do this often?"

"Yeap, as you do too, I guess."

"What are you? Some kind of whore?"

"How is my sleeping around any worse than your sleeping around Jakob?"

"I am a man!"

"Then you are a man whore, according to your logic."

That was too much for Jakob, he gave me a dirty look, picked up his coat and slammed the door behind him. Bang! How dare a woman give herself men prerogatives?

If I had not bedded Jakob right away I might have found out too late what an arrogant diva he was.

A sunny afternoon of 1995, Leila and I were having a curry in town when we spotted absolute perfection, eating his meal a couple of tables away from us. A real show stopper, Dorian looked like a Viking, golden blond hair, sky blue eyes, perfect teeth, sexy pout, golden skin, muscles bulging everywhere. Since Leila and I were both single at that time, we entertained very naughty thoughts about the Viking and wondered which one of us should go for him. Was he gay? Was he a model? Was he single? Would he like us? Was he maybe too good looking to want to sleep with either of us? When he walked to the cigarette machine and back we were practically panting; tall, feline, sex on legs. Leila wondered how she could date him and I was wondering how fast I could get him into my bed/ coffee table/ rug/toilet seat... anywhere.

My friend and I played rock, scissor and paper to know who would give it a try. I won. Cheekily I walked over Dorian's table with both our business cards and smiled.

"May I sit down? I asked once I was seated. Excuse me, I just have to tell you that my friend Leila and I find you drop-dead gorgeous and wonder if you would consider having a one night stand with either of us."

I bat my eyelashes at this perfect Greek statue until he nonchalantly took both business cards off my hand with a sexy wink and answered in a even sexier voice:

"I'll have you on Monday afternoon and your friend on Wednesday night, that's the only free time I got.

Cool?"

"You got it", I gasped and returned to my table to a red faced Leila who couldn't believe what I had just done.

"Did you just go to that hottie to tell him we want to shag him?" she whispered furiously.

"But Leila, that was the plan!"

"Are you insane? I should have known that this is something you would think nothing of doing! How do you feel now that he's told you to get lost?"

She assumed the hot Viking had rejected me!

"I don't know how that would feel because I have a date with him on Monday and you on Wednesday".

"???????????????????" Leila thought.

"Yes, I confirmed, he likes us both."

"But this man is absolute perfection and we are not exactly looking like top models."

"Who cares? I laughed, maybe he likes confidant women."

Leila backed out of the deal because she found the whole thing a little too weird but I slept with beautiful blond vikinglike Dorian. His technique was superb; his body looked like it had been sculpted by a very skilled artist. There had to be something wrong with him. I found it out during the post sex conversation. Dorian kept talking about his modelling career, the silicone implants in his pectorals and calves (*aha! I knew it*), what shampoo he used to make his hair even more golden and, and,

and. I was so bored with this Greek statue that I asked him to leave, pretending I had to get up early. He too needed his beauty sleep in order to keep looking gorgeous... did he tell me he was a model? Yes he did, thank you, could he leave now please. Thank you. Thank you for not coming back you bore, I thought.

How embarrassing! I had slept with a perfect bimbo. Leila had a good laugh about it and we even had a nickname for Dorian whenever we saw him in town. As far as we were concerned he was known as "Sois beau et tais-toi", meaning "shut up and be beautiful". Doesn't it sound cuter in French?

I'm so glad Dorian was only a one night stand, how awful it would have been to keep dating him only to get attached to an empty self loving Greek statue?

More recently, I met a man who was the embodiment of what I love to play with. Dragan was tall, muscular without being bulgy, circumcised, dark, bald, strong features, big nose, intense black eyes and extremely kissable lips. A strong silent type, a man of few words, neither smart nor simple. I already figured he was a dominant macho but I had to have him. My new target was responsive when I made a pass at him in an airport souvenir shop. We had a drink and before he would board his plane I told him I wished to have a wonderful one night stand with him should he ever return to this country. He gave me a slight kiss and said he wasn't leaving until the next day anyway. Yes! When he booked a room for us, I was beyond excited! I can truly say that Dragan was the best one night stand in the history of great one night stands. It felt surreal to be in the arms of this amazing man from a world so different to mine, what was he going to be like? He stepped out of the shower wrapped in a white towel: so gorgeous! He was perfect. He wasn't fucking, he was making love. And lots of it! This is one of the two men in my life who has been able to reach the top of my profound womanhood, I couldn't get enough and nor could he. Pure madness had me scream his name as he kept giving me multi orgasms all night and most of the morning. I put my brain on pause and just gave in to the waves of pleasure we surfed on until it was time for Dragan to leave.

The conversation we had during breakfast confirmed what I already suspected: dominant, controlling, bossy, asking many questions without ever answering any. Part of me was sorry Dragan was returning to Bosnia but my brain rejoiced to have him out of my life because falling for a man like Dragan can only lead to heartache and misery. We didn't even exchange numbers for we knew a one night stand was all destiny would let us give each other and we were fine with that. Also it wouldn't surprise me if he had a wife and a couple of mistresses in Bosnia, which meant I would keep my hands off Dragan anyway. Messing with married men is against my sexual ethic. I was blessed to know such a perfect one night stand with such a hottie.

I was very fortunate not to be needy, clingy or involved with such a macho.

All these sex experiences make me think that one night stands are the best. You don't waste time on someone who would turn out to be tyrannical, irresponsible, arrogant, unloving or worse. The best sex ever with any man in any relationship is the first night. I often walked away from a relationship thinking what a pity I didn't stop it after the first night. At least I would have fond memories of him. On a first night, a man does his very best to impress you. His primal instincts are to make you remember him as the best ever! After a million nights together he couldn't care less about your opinion and it either turns into tenderness or indifference. We all know this deep down, so why do we all keep making the same mistakes? Even I can't answer this.

One night stands are not only exciting and adrenalin pumping; there is also a sure thing. You get immediate satisfaction without going through the boring ritual of endless dinners and pointless conversations, pretending to get to know each other when in fact you want the same thing. To rip each other's clothes off and dive into the new adventure.

Sometimes a one night stand is so wonderful, so compelling that you keep going back for more and it can develop into a nice "sexual friendship" where the two of you meet every so often for the sole purpose of having passionate sex with no strings attached and then peacefully return to your real life with a smile on your face and a song in your heart. This has happened to me with Byron, Mark, Volker, Djawad, Karim, Igor... Hmm, nice! However not all one night stands are revelations, sometimes something goes wrong and you find out post sex that he is arrogant, selfish, racist or worse. In such cases you will be greatly relieved to know this.

You see? One night stands do save time when they are on your own terms. You could have wasted so much time and energy trying to understand the guy, to help him, to fix him maybe? Now you are able to make a decision not to have anything to do with the pig again. This means you have gained considerable time and avoided a huge dose of disappointment. How cool is that?

8.   Is cyber sex cheating?

I used to think that if you had a partner you were physically faithful to, it was perfectly alright to fool around on the net with people you would never meet in real life. If there is no physical contact, I thought, it did not count as cheating.

Right?

Wrong.

After having experienced it a few times with a friend who was stuck faraway for months, I beg to differ. Cyber sex with others than your partner definitely is cheating.

Why?

Because it is real fun, real emotions, real giggles, sometimes even real pleasure, though it does not even compare to physical sex. Lying about it and covering it up also is real lying. The excitement of looking forward to your cyber date and checking your watch or your screen for your cyber sex buddy is real, as is the frustration when the session is interrupted or over.

I was introduced to the world of cyber sex by a cute guy I met on a social network. He had asked me to install a webcam on my laptop and I did because I wanted to see his face. I will never forget how good this felt the first time, I had seen pictures of him before but I was seduced by his handsome face and his boyish charm. Little did I know that he was a porn addict and soon we were striping for each other with him telling me how to touch, where to touch. *"Could he get a close up? Could he see my face as I (pretended) to come? Did I like what he was showing me?"* It was a lot of fun until I got frustrated and we couldn't resist meeting face to face. But that's another story.

The problem with those cyber connections is that women actually think they have some kind of relationship with their cyber lovers and feel lost and confused when those connections are brutally severed from one day to the next without a word of explanation. To men it is clearly just a play tool and they can have several cyber lovers at once.

I don't regret my experience even though we are no longer on talking terms, but I refuse to do this again as I have realized cybersex can get hard to keep under control. But I will tell you this: the power of cyber sex is borderline addictive. Waiting for your cyber lover to get online is as bad as sitting by the phone waiting for a real lover to call. Demeaning and frustrating is what it is.

Remembering what he had made me feel does entitle me to declare that yes, cyber sex can be powerfully pleasurable. Therefore, if your man or your woman is cyber shagging someone else on the net while you are cooking or working, you are being cheated on and you are right to be just as hurt and humiliated as if they had had a mistress in your own bed!

9. Djawad, the Yoruba warrior

Djawad (name changed) was a phenomenal looking black man in his late thirties. He came from Nigeria and belonged to an old ethnic group called the Yorubas. Traditionally they were warriors, polygamists, intelligent, hard working and irresistible... like my Djawad was. He wanted me as soon as we met, but had no ideas he couldn't dominate me the way Nigerian men do their women.

Very tall, very strong, his voice sounded like a rapper on acid and his skin was like chocolate silk. We had a beautiful connection, we always met at his apartment and he would cook awesome African meals for me, then we would have a cuddle and a talk in front of a movie before going to bed. I can truly say that was one of the best lover I've ever had. Huge but gentle. And soooo long lasting.

However, some cracks started to appear within a few weeks. He didn't like to kiss and he hated giving oral sex but was very happy to be the recipient of it. But what really annoyed me is that he kept telling me to keep quiet! Who keeps quiet during good sex? Had he never seen a woman come before?

At first I thought he was joking but I realised he wasn't when he would whisper *shut up* each time I would start to voice my pleasure. I tried to confront Djawad about this, but he was embarrassed to discuss sex. Whenever we were somewhere public he would let go of my hand at the first sight of a black person. After the millionth time this happened, I pointed out that if I were openly dating a black man in a white country, he had no business being closeted about dating a white woman. Djawad denied doing this and insisted it was my imagination getting the best of me. Ladies, when your man tell you it is not him, it is your imagination playing tricks on you, it is time to leave; not only is he lying but he is disrespecting you.

I wanted to give Djawad a chance but his jealousy and third degree questionings of my whereabouts were progressively eroding my patience. I agreed to watch Nigerian movies in order to understand his culture better and I wasn't very pleased with what I saw in each movie: married men constantly cheating on their wives and all their mistresses but not tolerating a single moment of cheating from said mistresses; men having lots of children with many different lovers, legally; rich people having poor people prostrating before them; employers making their employees call them "masters"; voodoo practiced wantonly to get into other people's pants against their knowledge. My goodness! Was that for real?

Why my Yoruba thought I would approve of this, I will never know. I didn't even try to point out the absurdity of this behaviour, hoping that those movies were only caricatures and not actual.

It came to the end when one evening Djawad insisted I come to see him, although I really didn't want to because I had to get up at six the next morning for a weeklong trip abroad. Against my better judgement, I went along and we had some yummy African food in front of the television. After I did the dishes, I became quite amorous on the couch but he wouldn't respond. I did all I could to arouse him but he gently pushed me away saying he really wanted to see the end of this car race, why didn't I go to bed and wait for him there? Pffff. I put on a skimpy black nightie and purred I was waiting for him in bed.

I got into his red sheets and... fell asleep ! I woke up alone and freezing at four o'clock in the morning. Where was he? I walked in on him watching porn. That was it! I went back to his bedroom to put my clothes back on then returned to the leaving room to yell at him. Who watches porn on TV when you have a woman in your bed? And what the hell was I doing here if he was staying away from me all night? I couldn't believe what I was hearing:

"Baby, what's wrong with you? It's all in your mind. What are you doing getting dressed at 4 am? Do you really want to walk the street with high heels at this time? Don't be like that and go back to bed."

Was the dude mentally challenged or was that a power play? The power Djawad imagined his penis had.

"Would you mind telling me why I'm here? If it was about eating in front of the television and snoring alone in bed, I could have done that at home, at least I would have had the loving company of my cats. Why am I here tonight if you don't want sex?" I demanded to know.

"Baby, there is more to a relationship that just bang bang." He said.

"After twenty years of marriage maybe, not after only six months of dating!" I shouted.

I was so angry Djawad had purposely wasted an entire night of my life for a display of power. I told him what to do with his macho power games and slammed the door on my way out. I did wait for a couple of minutes, hoping he would follow me, apologize and drag me back to bed for some great make up sex but he didn't. In fact he felt offended that I had been so unladylike (read untameable) and had no idea why I was fuming. I got home at almost 5 am, had a nice long cuddle with my cats and found solace in their purring.

Over the years, I forgave Djawad, even reconnected with him sexually a couple of time but it never worked out because he wants a lover who is his companion and he truly doesn't understand what a sexual friendship is.

Something tells me that he would however completely grasp the concept of having a faithful girlfriend while he would "spread his seed" all over town.

10. Liquid fire Mark

Mark (name changed) was another gorgeous Nigerian man who was much more open to European ways that my Yoruba had been.

Mark is very tall, (why do I attract giants?), very black and has the most enchanting smile. His body is a magnificent ebony statue and his love making skills send, what I can only describe as shots of liquid fire up and down my legs until my toes. He loves spooning in between two rounds, he is incredibly cuddly but I wish he would last longer. He blames it on the condoms but I refuse to stop using them. One day Mark suggested we both get tested so that we can go bareback. Not an option.

"Why is it not an option baby? I dont fuck around." he pleaded.

"Oh but I do." I replied.

The dreaded discussion was coming up. Mark wanted to know why I would need to sleep around when I had a lover like him. I asked if he remembered our first date when we clearly established neither of us wanted a relationship.

"Ancient history, he shrugged, by now we know each other well."

And the more he knew me the more he realised I was wife material: loving, caring, smart, hardworking and organized. How did he figure that out? The man who had failed two marriages wondered if the woman who equally failed two marriages, would make a fine third wife! Did Mark say that for me to lower my guards? Was it a con to make me go bareback? Failed on both accounts. Another time Mark assured me that he would make his next wife so happy that she won't even need another man.

Why don't men understand I get bored quickly with the same guy around? I don't fool around because I'm not satisfied, *au contraire*, I fool around for the fun of discovering new lovers, novel sensations, novel experiences. New, new, new! It is the chase that turns me on, the novelty, not the routine. Routine with a great man is dangerous. Routine leads to trust, feelings, love: an open invitation to be hurt and an ugly fear of losing him. I won't go through this heartache again.

Mark once surprised me by waiting by the main door as I was leaving work one late afternoon and he really turned on the charm. We walked back to my place holding hands, showing he had no problem with openly dating white women. He was lovely, romantic and irresistible. Back at my place, my cat actually hissed at him.

"That can't be a good sign" I thought. We embarked on an ocean of volupty for half an hour. Later on, as Mark was getting dressed, he asked me why I don't want to get married again. I sat up in bed, wrapped my sheets around me and pretended not to look as annoyed as I really felt.

"Honey where does that come from anyway? Are we not having fun? Why would you want change that?"

Now he was getting seriously challenged.

"Look, I have had my fun now I want to settle down, I want to come home to my own woman who will ask me how my day has been, I want to eat the food she'll cook for me, I want to be cuddled, I want to be loved. How hard is that to understand?"

I knew this would be leading to a break up but I did try to reason Mark because I liked him a lot.

"Mark, I was honest with you, I didn't pretend to be who I am, in the hope of landing a husband. I'm not good at marriage and I certainly don't want any more children. Besides I'm fifteen years older than you are. This can't happen. Wasn't I clear on what I had to offer you?"

Men! They always want the opposite of what you have to give them. Had I been a nice girl with dreams of a white wedding and quiet family meals, I'm pretty sure Mark would have run away.

"But you have so much more to offer than just that! He insisted. Or do you really think I'm not good enough for you? My father is a diplomat, I have a college degree, I have never been to prison or in a gang or whatever it is black men are supposed to do. How in the world do you find me not good enough for the likes of you!" he shouted at me.

Was it what it was about? Because he was black?

"Come on, I pleaded with him, if a black man is good enough to be my lover he is certainly good enough to be my boyfriend or my husband but I want to remain single, just like I have always maintained all trough our relationship. Sure I could give more but I have given up on love long ago and you are not forcing me on that road again. You have no idea what this means to me to be the boss of my life. Can't we just carry on?"

Mark's blackberry rang; he quickly looked at it without picking it up.

"You see this? he pointed to his blackberry, this is a really decent white woman ,who wants me and she doesn't have your issues with relationships and marriage. Unless you give me a reason not to, I will drive up to her house tonight and then... who knows."

There we were again, if I had a dollar every time a man gave me this ultimatum, I would drive a Maserati by now. I sat there silently as Mark put on his jacket and slammed the door on his way out after giving me one last questioning look.

How I hate those moments, but my commitment to singlehood and independence are well worth it.

No regrets.

11. Black magic, Brahim

It had been so long since I held a black man in my arms that I practically jumped on the gorgeous Senegalese who was checking some massage books in the natural medicine section of my favourite store. Brahim had recently returned from a trip to India where he had trained in tantric massage and meditation. I was thrilled when he suggested to meet on the following evening. A man with that kind of knowledge is definitely worth spending an evening with.

My heart was throbbing as I knocked on Brahim's door.

Did he have something seductive in mind for little old me?

What a feast for the eyes! There must have been two dozen candles of all colours and sizes burning all over his living room as well as some African chanting on the stereo. My new black lover asked me to lie down on the floor with my clothes off and on top of silky yellow sheets. I started striping off, cheekily looking at him and trying to keep in tempo with Yousso N'Dour's voice that filled the whole place with an extremely erotic atmosphere. I kept maintaining eye contact and stood there in red lace bra and panties trying to look as this was my everyday look and not the results of a trip to the sauna, a facial, some waxing and lotioning that took up my entire afternoon. Brahim liked what he saw.

Have you ever noticed how men look when they are

about to have sex? They appear all dignified and cool but their inner teenage boy is jumping up and down with joy, screaming: "YAY! I'm gonna get laid! I'm gonna get laid! Woohoohoo I'm gonna get laid!" Their eyes are shining with anticipation, their pulses race, they can barely talk or if they do they utter some nonsense or they mumble, their breathing is shallow, their mouths go dry. They are nervous and relaxed at the same time. What goes on in a man's head just before he makes love? Anxiety, fear, overwhelming? Victorious that they are getting the female at last? I certainly hope they are not wondering who has been there before and are they going to be better that the last guy.

For now Brahim sported a hot "I'm gonna have a great fuck" look on his face and he motioned for me to lie down. I did. He dipped his fingers in some powerfully enchanted scented oil and treated me to a wonderful sensuous body massage while my lingerie put on a disappearing act. I loved it when Brahim ripped my red panties off my body with his perfect teeth. Could he be sexier?

His mobile phone rang.

"Honey? Are you gonna pick that phone up or let it ring all night?"

"What phone? I'm not hearing any phone ringing, right now I am in another world" he smiled. *Tu m as maraboutè*" (You put a spell on me)

What a charming thing to say, I can't imagine a white man coming up with such a cute line. Can you?

Nevertheless Brahim still sounded like a man who had something to hide... Don't they all?

After a while of being so pampered I didn't hear the phone ring anymore. I was in a whirl of novel sensations. Brahim's large black hands on my white skin were such a turn on. The lasciviousness of African chanting, the plush cushions everywhere, the intoxicating power of the mixed oils he was now caressing my legs with. His eyes were closed; he was slowly humming to himself. It was as if he were having a mystical experience while exploring me... and he started to really explore further and further.

The whole set up was driving me wild with desire I just wanted Brahim inside but he was so into discovering every inch of me that I had to let him be in charge. At some point I thought I was going to explode when suddenly he ever so softly whispered in my ear:

"Tu veux?" (Do you want?)

Are you kidding me? Of course I want to! I could scream, that's how much I want to. I want to now! I've been wanting to for a couple of hours ! Instead I just sighed

"Oui" I breathed in and out. "Oui, je veux" (Yes I want it)

Later on, we were lying on the floor, entangled into each other. As soon as my brain got working again, I purred to the man who had given me the most seductive date of my life, that this had been beyond fabulous. He smiled a large happy grin and said:

"I know."

And he was modest as well! Brahim justified himself by saying that when sex is good between two people it will be good anywhere, in the kitchen, on the toilet seat or even in the garden's tool shed. I have to admit I'm not too sure about the toilet seat bit. Brahim made a few gestures above my face and thorax to balance my chakras after the energetic storm my body had just enjoyed. If I didn't know about Chinese energetic and chakras, what you just did would have freaked me out a little. I told him.

"But you do know about it, I saw you checking the same books I was."

Brahim never asked any question and even drove me home. What a gentleman.

Magic and multi orgasms followed by a non invasion of my privacy. Could a girl ask for more? Not this girl. I came home from my black magic date a little dizzy and giddy and now I was the one with a "I just had a great fuck" look on my face.

12. The London Shagathon, Joey

About three years ago, I had a boredom phase. There was nothing new to shag in Zurich. I got so bored of the same guys calling and of calling the same guys. Could it be that I had dated everything datable in Zurich? Probably. If you leave out the gays, the married men, the men my age, I guess I had been dating everything that moved in my city and I wanted something new. Trouble is there was nothing new to shag. Oops, was I ever going to get laid again? Out of sheer curiosity I did something I had never done before... I checked out an international dating website. I scrolled over all the usual liars who pretend they want a relationship so that they can get naive women to give them hopeful sex. Something caught my attention. A black man in London was giving a brief description of himself: smart, articulate and good in bed. What followed was even more appealing, "no string attached Joey". That was his pseudo and he invited any female who wanted it, to spend a fabulous weekend in London, eating, sightseeing and having lots and lots of great sex with no strings attached! He insisted he was allergic to relationships and just wanted a sexual exchange with a hot stranger; nothing else. That sounded good and I emailed no-string-attached Joey that same day. We began emailing each other regularly. He pretended he was a paralegal from a posh London area and I pretended to believe it because I was not interested in building any connection with him. His emails were both fun and sexy and we finally decided on a weekend that was convenient for both of us. I arranged a baby sitter for my cat and off I went. Since half my family is English I do know London quite well but I thought it would be fun to let Joey think he was actually showing me something new. Feelings of guilt washed over me as I embarked on the Eurotrain in Paris. I had never been to England without visiting relatives. In fact nobody even knew I was there except for my best friends. This was something I was doing for myself, I thought. I work hard all year and I'm a good person. Surely it is ok to give myself a little treat, to do something that is not work related or service related, to do something a little unusual just for me for once. We had arranged to meet in this pub and when he turned up I was not at all impressed by his looks or his clothes. However I decided to follow him to his apartment because I know that the best lovers are not the cutest ones. He took my hand as we left the taxi and walked into what really looked like a council building. Once in his living room I admired the rows of books and the graduation photos. I discreetly checked a couple of envelopes and learned that he had lied about his name, hmm, not good. He spoke with a strong Jamaican accent, which makes me think he probably lied about his job too, but who cared? I wasn't there to inspect him.

The weekend itself was fabulous. Joey was not only absolutely fabulous in bed, well endowed and tireless, he also cooked fantastic Jamaican dishes for me and showed me Piccadilly Circus, Knightsbridge and Buckingham Palace. We also had an extraordinary sex marathon or should I say a shaggathon. We had a bubble bath and shagged, we started watching a movie, re-shagged. We went out for a walk and run back to his place to shag again. We fell asleep after intense shagging and shagged again as we woke up, and after breakfast, and after lunch and, and, and, and... Until I had to leave.

Wow! I fell asleep on the Eurotrain home, achy but so very satisfied. A sex marathon in London with a hot stranger was exactly what I had needed and since Joey was not interested in relationship I didn't even have to deal with lies and deceptions afterwards neither did he. I went back to London twice!

A few months later, Joey contacted me , insisting he really wanted to repeat the magic of those shaggathons, I was so stressed out that I had no time off to travel so I suggested Joey come here to Zurich from Friday to Sunday so that it wouldn't change my planning and we had all weekend to shag like crazy. Big mistake. When am I gonna learn my lesson? Never, ever, follow up an out of town one night stand, never! What happens in Paris or in London or Milan stays in Paris, London or Milan. This kind of magic cannot be repeated, the expectations are too high. Joey came on that Friday and told me he could stay until Wednesday. What?

But Joey I have a job and a few social commitments that I can't cancel!

"Yo man, that's ok; I will just walk around and take pics."

The first couple of days were great, we went dancing and Joey couldn't believe how many beautiful women were all alone and without an escort, in London you have to practically queue up for a woman who is by herself, he said. We had tons of really good sex. After the sexual thrill was gone, I saw some sides to Joey that I disliked. He would look at my book shelves and didn't like any of the authors I did, he had in fact brought a Clive Barker novel to read. He was scared of my cat that made it a game of making him jump by simply walking towards him and staring silently. What is it with most black men and cats? On the first day I had cooked spaghetti with tuna, which he loved. On the second day I made some cevap cicip, an Albanian spicy meat dish, and he complained that he didn't like it as much as my spaghettis! Would I mind cooking it again every day he was here? Would I! My education stopped me from saying what an ungrateful capricious macho he was. Not only did I cook for a man, something I only did to return the favour, but he was criticising my choice in cooking! What an idiot. Could it get any more unpleasant? It could. It did.

By Monday night we were all shagged out and had absolutely nothing to talk about. Joey went out for a walk. I was grateful for the silence and enjoyed watching a French movie with my purring cat. At around midnight Joey called to say he had met some black guys and they were playing billiard, I shouldn't wait for him to have dinner! Now he was taking me for granted. Of course I had had dinner a couple of hours before but I resented his rudeness.

Oh dear, I was letting a guy into my life for five minutes and he was already behaving as if he were in conquered territory. When Joey came back I pretended to be too sleepy to talk or to have sex. Next day we barely talked and we certainly didn't have sex either. My cat and I were so relieved to see him pack his bags and even happier when he left earlier than scheduled for the airport. After that, I never took Joey's calls again, I wasn't about to repeat this boring experience again. I love being single, if only to avoid this kind of stressful situation when a man takes you for granted and gets in your way of life.

13. Once you go black...or do you really?

Wh e all know that old saying... Once you go black, you can never go back.

I have always wondered why people say that. Many women I know are afraid to experiment with black men because they think they will never be satisfied with a white man again. Let me tell you from experience that nothing could be further from the truth. On a planet with such racial diversity, why should we give ourselves such limits? Sleeping with only white men, or only black men or only with red heads seems very frustrating to me. The truth is all men are sexy, all men have something wonderful to offer if they are into you. Blacks, whites, Asians, Latinos, biracial, bisexual, disabled, valid, all men are worth checking out. What a pity to know only one kind of lovers when there is so much for us to explore.

Everybody who knows me personally will tell you that I prefer black men. I love my black men and came out of the closet long ago. The silky skin, the firm muscles, the warm smiles, the deep voices, the charming confidence, the moves, the beautiful contrast of our skin colours when we are sweating together are pure delight. However, I will not hesitate to invite a Chinese or a Caucasian in my bed if he is sexy, funny, warm, smart and knows how to turn me on. It is not the colour of a man that makes him irresistible but rather his sex appeal, his aura.

The sexiness of a man is in the way he moves, how he looks at you, the words he uses, his confidence, his nonchalance, if he makes you laugh, if he makes you feel good before he even touches you. And this is not a matter of colour; it is entirely individual and regardless of his looks, credo or social conditions.

Black men, black Americans, British, Europeans and Africans are not only fabulous lovers, they also love to cook for their women, they are fans of talking and giggling as long as you want to. They are often, not always, but often very well endowed and can make love for hours without using Viagra or snorting coke. But they are not happy about giving oral sex, though they love receiving it.

They are very cuddly and kissy but after a few dates they will want a real relationship, wishing for you to commit and be faithful while finding it perfectly acceptable to still date other women.

Africans are specially demanding that way and very naughty. African men will be horrified if you cheat on them but conveniently forget their own dalliances with others. White men may not go on for hours but most of them love going down on women even if they are just one night stands but white men cringe at the word relationship, convenient for me but not for all. White men will only cook for you if they really are into you. Latinos are nonstop fun, dancing, laughing, having sex. They already know it won't get serious and don't pretend otherwise, Ahhh you've got to love Latinos, just don't fall in love with one because Latinos don't even acknowledge the existence of the word monogamy.

Bisexual men are really interesting to play with, they are adventurous and non-committal, just don't demand that they chose one gender over another.

Disabled men are as capable of giving pleasure as valid men and they all have profound and intelligent personalities well worth knowing, just be **honest** with them and **don't** toy with their feelings. Have I got my point across?

There is good and bad points in all sort of men and there are all fascinating. The only way you don't "come back " from a man is if you both fall in love, but that is another story.

All men are worth dating. If you only go for physically perfect "Greek statues" you will be bored beyond belief. Therefore, once you go black.... of course you can come back and return and come back again and come again, go back on White lane or Latino street before diving into Black sea and return.

So go for it, explore everybody as much as you like and enjoy the rides.

Let's ignore preconceived prejudices.

14. Am I grooming guys to become better men?

As we know, I decided to quit love years ago after my second husband broke my heart. I love the way I live now but it doesn't mean I never form some kind of bonds with the people I date. Some of them inspire something I would describe as feelings, especially the ones I dally with often. However I am very serious about the commitment I made to remaining single even if I am occasionally reminded of the price I am willing to pay for my independent man free, love free, life.

As intimacy builds up between a shag buddy and me, there are times where things get deeper, not just sexually. You start to talk about your lives; you even council and comfort each other. You compare notes on life's many important issues like children, career and health. Sometimes you may even have a hard time letting go and you will be hugging and kissing good night by the door a little longer than you should. I often get some flash backs on the next day, thinking about how fantastic last night was or how seductively he moves his hips, or that thing he does with his tongue, or the scent on his skin that you love breathing in when your face is in his neck and that vein pulsating on his forehead when he comes, his voice when he screams, his...

Ok! Move on now!

That's what I always tell myself to snap out of these

lovely reveries. Whenever I feel like sending a nice text to a lover I like, I will resist the impulse and send a saucy one instead. So what should have been: *my lips are bruised from your wonderful kisses last night* which is way too romantic, becomes: *hmm I can still taste you,*

What a fantastic fuck last night! This is my way of saying: *Sure I like you, I like you a lot but it is purely sexual, nothing else, tenderness and loving are not part of the deal mister.*

I have even been known to escape away from wonderful guys I knew I could lose control with. Sabotaging the budding relationship by being obnoxious to someone I actually had strong feelings for. I always double lock the door to my heart to make sure whoever he is cannot ever get in against my will.

I regularly get dumped by a shag buddy whenever the time comes when they will want something more that I'm not willing to give. They walk out.

Some try to dominate me and tell me what to do, I refuse to comply. They walk out too.

The dreaded talk is almost always the same:

You and I get on well, you make me feel wonderful, you really know how to make a man feel special, you and I have a good thing going, boring, boring boring, you are girl friend material, boring, boring boring, If you don't want what I have to offer someone else will, who do you think you are anyway! It happened three times in 2010 alone. After the closure of our sexual friendship, most of those men end up marrying or living with the very next girl they date after me. I'm thinking of this cute Italian I saw for months, when it became inevitable to either get involved or break up, he broke up and the next time I run into him he wore a ring and held hand with his pregnant wife. (But when I run into him into my favourite salsa club a few weeks ago he made a pass at me never the less).

Mark walked out furiously, wondering why I figured out he was not good enough for me. I saw Mark last month, proudly holding hands with an unsuspecting beautiful black woman. Byron who always complained that I only called him for sex had now settled with a cute blonde and I am happy, for Byron deserves a good woman who commits. Pavel, a hot blond, forever swinging from a "lets a have a shag fest" mode to a "I want to be loved" mode, is now living with his fiancée who is blissfully unaware that the whole city of Zurich, men and women included, have revisited Kama Sutra with her man. Djawad the hottest Yoruba in town told me he wants a girlfriend who does the dishes after they ate the meal he's cooked for them. So yes, they might have been ready for commitments after a while but I don't like being pressured and I certainly never want to belong to one man in particular. Never again. Let those who want to have those men have them and be happy with them.

There are so many, many wonderful men of all kind that have so much to offer. I would hate to miss out on hot sex with no strings attached with a cute stranger just because I would have pledged loyalty to my own man. Since infidelity and open relationships are not an option for me, I prefer to remain single.

Singlehood is the right way for my sexual happiness. What will happen when I will get old and no longer desirable enough to cruise for sex? Well I will feed on my funny sexy memories and take up knitting or home jam making to spoil my future grand children with. Or I could run a shelter for cats. After all everybody says I must have been a cat in my previous life...

My friends think I'm taking defence mechanism a little too far. Maybe I am. But it is worth it to keep the life I lead now. Don't you feel sorry for me, this is what I do, this is who I am. And I love it.

15. Men screwing us into submission

Domination needs not always be violent and painful. A clever man will be more subtle when establishing dominion over his woman. How can a man dominate us without using brutality? Simply by giving us lots and lots of great sex, until we are almost addicted to his body, until we cannot even think for ourselves. Many men try to screw us into submission. What possesses them to do such a thing? Who will ever know what goes on in their mind? They just do, that's all.

Let me give some examples.

- A man who gets his wife pregnant to stop her going to college and get a higher degree than he has.

- A man who only sporadically gives his wife good sex to keep her panting for him, always wanting more.

- A man who forces his woman to perform sexual favours against her will, knowing this will tear her soul apart.

- A man who never makes love when she wants to, just to show her he is in charge.

A man like that is nothing but an unsecure caveman.

I have had some men who would try to tire me out in bed just before they had to take a trip away, in the hope that I wouldn't have the energy to bed another man in their absence.

This is not desire; this is an abominable need to control your sexuality. A man who shags you frantically for hours with the sole scope of making sure their "territory" will not be letting another penis in, is indeed a control freak. If they want exclusivity, why don't they just ask for it? Or could it be because they have no desire to reciprocate it?

What about the man who jumps on his woman just to stop her to go out with her friends? Or the one who starts petting you heavily when you are talking on the phone to your boss? Some men will sacrifice their bodies only to change our minds or to slow us down. Fortunately it no longer works on me, but only because I'm aware some men use their sexuality to dominate and control us. That's me, but how about you?

Ladies, please stop giving in just because your man gives it so good. In most cases he will have an agenda and will use great sex to make you do whatever he wants you to. This is extremely manipulative and self serving, where is the fun in that?

If you show your man you love sex with him but will not allow him to rule your life, two things can happen. Either he will decide you are too strong for him to tame and he will move to the next victim: good riddance. Or he will respect you and give you great sex only because he loves it.

Many of my shag buddies have tried to screw me into submission, mainly to force me into an unwanted relationship I had clearly said no to. I remember a really hot Latino one night stand who asked me between kisses if I were ready to make a sacrifice for him! I got so scared I jumped on my clothes and never spoke to the creep again. Maybe he meant it as something playful but the word sacrifice is not a word to be toying with and I was immediately turned off.

A gorgeous Czechoslovakian would automatically throw himself at me each time I mentioned I had to go away somewhere with my friends.

A hot Albanian once tried to impose his wife on me; he found we had so much in common, the three of us could be quite happy together.

Djawad had the audacity to let me sleep alone in his bed while he watched telly in another room, just for a power trip.

Karim, my regular stalker could not understand why I never fell in love with him after years of absolutely fabulous sex, even my second husband would ask me to go buy him some croissants at six in the cold morning because, after all he had just given me a nice fuck. The list goes on and on but I'm sure you got the picture by now. All those men threaten to take their penises away if we don't do as we are told whatever their requests might be. Who do they think they are? Who are they indeed to have so little respect for their bodies and for our intelligence?

Do men really think that occasionally giving us a couple of orgasms entitles them to some kind of power over us? Apparently they do. We just need to fight back and refuse to be screwed into submission.

Yes, some men are hard to walk away from and even harder to get over, but it doesn't mean we should forget who we are and what we want out of our lives.

If you are a woman in this situation, please don't let your man rule you just because he is wonderful, don't forget that you are wonderful too and a relationship based on blackmail is not a relationship at all.

16. You cannot help a self destructive man, Carlos

Carlos (name changed) was a witty, sexy and very charismatic Portuguese bartender. He hit on me straight away when we met nine years ago. I have tried to occult this truly inglorious affair but it might help you ladies to learn something vital:

YOU CANNOT HELP A SELF DESTRUCTIVE MAN WHO DOESNT WANT TO BE HELPED!

What that big enough? Did you all see it?

Ok, here is what happened.

For some reason I was feeling a little vulnerable that summer, so when this hottie went out of this way to make a pass at me, I asked him to meet me on the following day. It was the first of August, a Swiss national holiday that involves time off, big street parties and more fireworks than the French 14th of July and the American 4th of July.

On that first date Carlos impressed me with mind-blowing sex; even the fireworks outside didn't compare!

Everything about him was attractive: his sense of humour, his mischievousness, his incredible sexual appetite. I had never been the recipient of toe sucking before and though he was not very big where size does matter, he took me on whirls of orgasmic twisters.

We used to play with food. Carlos would drop a

dollop of fresh cream on my knee to lick it, working his way up. He would bite into an orange before going down on me, we would shower together, bathe while savouring chocolate dipped strawberries... delicious kinky stuff.

He loved brushing my hair, which he had asked me to keep long, he enjoyed watching me dress. As you see it started really well... Until one day I discovered that Carlos had quite a drinking problem!

Since my new shag buddy refused to be kept in the closet like a good shag buddy should, we used to go out all the time, shopping, clubbing and holding hands. It was getting out of control, but I saw it too late. Two months of intensive dating later, I found out that he was not only an alcoholic but a coke user as well.

Could this get any worse? It could and it did. His dealer once threatened me because my big heart tried to get Carlos off drugs. Another time his dealer offered him a free gram of Columbian coke in exchange for a roll in the hay with me, when I was presented with this abomination, I slapped him so hard he fell on the floor. Words cannot describe how disgusted I felt and how embarrassed I was to have hit a person, but what annoyed me more is that I still lacked the strength to leave him. Did I mention he was still shagging his ex girlfriend behind my back and that he was sleeping around constantly while accusing me of infidelity? The girlfriend had really left because she wanted a baby and he didn't, now he wanted one with me and got upset when I explained I had already raised my children and wanted no more.

For some reason he was extremely jealous of my ex husband Jake and the fact that I bore him children. Showing him my birth control pills I explained again and again that I was happy to have grown teenagers now and there was no way I would go through the whole baby thing again. He didn't like that very much and we often argued about it.

I was very much into the silly bitch, so my heart of gold decided to save him. He agreed to try stopping drugs and booze on the condition that I would stay with him.

Those were crazy times when I was juggling two jobs, educating my two teenage children, running my household and separately keeping my guy on the straight and narrow. What was I thinking? Did I really think that I could stop an alcoholic bartender from drinking? How often did I pick him up from work, driving him back to his place, making sure he would have something to eat and get some sleep?

Whenever I wouldn't be willing to monitor him, Carlos would blackmail me emotionally, snort a week wages worth and complained it was my fault because I had ignored his needs. The blackmail would not always work, sometimes I would feel so relaxed at home with my family and our cats that I just couldn't be bothered with the drama queen and I would find the strength to say "*not tonight.*"

Other times he would get the upper hand and we would do risky things such as al fresco sex, which I do not recommend at all by the way. We once returned from a party at 5am and had sex in the train's toilets till the ticket controller knocked on the door to check our tickets. Not a very proud moment when the ticket controller gave me a dirty look. We did it everywhere: in the park, in the lift, in the laundry room. I was so afraid of getting caught, at the time it had been a major turn on, but later on I'd be crying in my shower wondering why I always gave in, although I had not really wanted to. Carlos in turn was resenting me for not letting him do drugs anymore; I did make it clear that I would leave him if he did again. We would fight and have fantastic make up sex afterwards.

One evening I switched my phone off as I was hosting an important family dinner and didn't want Carlos pestering me. Next morning at 6am I was queuing up at the baker for some freshly baked croissants to take home, when he jumped on me, red eyed and dishevelled. He was sleepless, high and irrational, screaming:

"Puta! Why did you leave me all alone? Were you with another man? Carlos is going to kill you Puta."

It took all my cold bloodied diplomacy to calm him down. There were a dozen people watching this and not one of them attempted to help. I almost expected those people to get the popcorn out while watching my hysterical aggressor making big gestures and screaming in my face. No one lifted a finger to help. It felt like being trapped in the bad part of a Tarentino movie where a bad man hurts the girl but she has more balls than he does. He kept on yelling at me. I just wanted it to stop, I wasn't prepared to be verbally aggressed any longer and I... slapped his face as hard as I could. Oh no! I raised my hand to someone again! That's how far he had pushed me.

His reaction was to smash the window of that bakery. Everybody run away quickly while I calmly asked him if he wanted to break up. After a string of *"Fucking Puta I'm going to kill you if leave Carlos!"* I escorted him back to his place so that he could sleep it off. That episode had shaken me to the core; we couldn't go on like this.

On the next evening he was again sobered up and charming. I gave him an ultimatum: drop the booze and the drugs right now, permanently, or we are through.

He seemed to understand and he did stop.

Now it was getting nice and sane, we would walk around in zoos and parks, he would marvel at the colour of the flowers, the leaves on trees, the songs of the birds. It was as he was discovering a brand new world he never knew existed. Hardly surprising when his own mother gave him his first joint at age fourteen. He noticed the beauty of the river and how fun it was to run or to play football. He had had no idea there was so much beauty to life without intoxication.

I had made it. Carlos was sober, he was saved. Yay for me! He was sober and felt extremely grateful to me for it.

All was well until he made the fatal mistake of telling his psychotic mother in Portugal about us and his sobriety. But mummy dearest did not want a happy healthy sober son; she wanted him to remain dependant, lonely and miserable like her drunken self.

Her manipulation began. She convinced Lourdes, his ex girlfriend, that he still loved her and that we were just a fling. The naive girl made a plea for Carlos and he fell for her «unconditional love» which included no restrictions on drinking and snorting. The evil mother knew Lourdes would never be strong enough to keep him sober, she also worked out that this would lead to our inevitable break up. It did. She also knew I would never take him back after he would again leave his ex, current and again ex girl friend. I didn't.

Her aim had been to have him all alone without any girlfriend to support him.

Exactly a year after our first date he stood me up to smoke a bong in a crack house, he broke up with me so brutally I cried for a week. Yes I cried, however I felt so loved by my family and my friends that I began to recover. On the eleventh day he was missing me already but the trust had been broken. Once I had left my mobile on my desk and my daughter picked it up to tell a shocked Carlos:

"Thank you for breaking up with my mom, now she can purge you out of her life at last. And by the way, you have just made the biggest mistake of your life because you will never find a class act like my mom again."

I was so moved when I found out what my daughter had done for me. Couldn't have been easy for her to talk to someone she despised that much. How sweet of her to defend me, her action gave me a lot of energy and I was able to start building myself up again.

Carlos kept hassling me for years, calling, threatening and texting but I was truly cured of him, eventually he had to go back to... drum rolls... his mother!

That's when I learned two valuable lessons in life. If you want to be rid of a bad man, just don't fuel the connection, never answer nor return his calls, emails or texts, just never answer them. Eventually he will move on to the next victim. My second revelation was that there is nothing you can do to help a self destructive man. If you meet one, just leave without a word, especially if the reasons for his state are deeply embedded in his past. Just get on with your life.

This was the most toxic relationship I have ever been in. Many toxic men have I dated before and after Carlos but nothing compares to that lowlife. He was so envious of my life, my lack of dependence to any crap, my great family, my wonderful friends, my exciting job, even of the beautiful friendship Jake and I share. The funny thing is this is how I met one of my long term shag buddy, Karim. He and Carlos had had a punch up about a professional disagreement and I had dragged Carlos away to safety.

By the time I saw Karim again we had something to talk about on our first date.

17. Taking control away from a bully

A sport therapist friend of mine had a scary encounter with a creepy footballer she was treating by herself, but she turned the situation around. Here is what happened.

Isabel was called out to give this footballer a strong sport massage because his legs were quite sore from overtraining and his regular therapist was out of town. As she arrived at the sport centre, my friend realised that the client was one she had refused to take on ever again after treating him only once. He had made her feel very uncomfortable, stared at her during the whole session as if she were a piece of meat and not a trained therapist. He had made a few innuendos without actually using rude words. She was relieved after he left and never took his calls after that. Now she was stuck as she didn't have a solid excuse to interrupt the session. The pig was smiling at her from his massage table knowing she couldn't back down and he was forcing her to touch him against her will.

Ambushed!

Isabel pretended not to remember him and behaved professionally. She asked a few questions about his type of pain, did he ice it, did he take anything and was he under a doctor's care, the usual routine. After questioning she told him to go shower and to lie down on his tummy, with his underwear on.

She started to handle his back while trying to ignore his ass moving ever slow slowly in a "would be" seductive way but not enough to be offensive. Again Isabel was stuck in an uncomfortable situation and she couldn't do a thing about it. When the time came for him to lie on his back, she stuck to the procedure and held up a large towel while looking away to protect his privacy. She covered him with the towel without looking down and again he had a disturbing creepy little flame in his eyes. Usually when clients get flirty all she has to do is apply more pressure on the points she handles and whatever went up quickly goes down. But this was an athlete with rock hard muscles, so hard and so trained that he welcomed the pressure.

As the therapist was working on his abs, the footballer was getting more and more aroused. An erection was starting to swell up underneath the thick towel. Isabel was humiliated, feeling almost victimised. Did I mention that they were all alone as everyone was away at lunch? The creepy client had the upper hand and was loving the fact that he made her so unsecure.

Things were looking bleak for my friend until she remembered who she was.

Isabel's friends always admired her courage and her fearlessness of men. Was she the kind of girl who would let a thug scare her like this? What would she advise a friend in the same predicament? Didn't she always say never tolerate blackmail and never bend to bullies?

Within moments she turned the situation around.

She took control.

She smiled at the bully and got aggressively seductive.

"What do you want?" she demanded to know.

The footballer mumbled, quite flabbergasted. Instead of cowering away from the menacing erection she went from victim to aggressor and roughly grabbed his manhood trough the towel with a firm hand.

"Is that what you want huh? A hand job?"

He didn't think it was much fun being on the wrong side of an aggression and said he would do it himself in the toilet if that was ok with her. He went away to wank off while she disinfected her hands thoroughly. Isabel picked up her briefcase and gave the now red faced bully one last glance that meant he better not trick her again.

It is as if the mere fact that demanding to touch his dick rather than dreading it, stopped the bully's budging violence. He became what he had wanted her to be: dirty and embarrassed.

Not only did Isabel turn a potentially dangerous situation in one that embarrassed the potential aggressor, but she took the control away from him. She took control and he went from intimidating bully to a sad wanker.

Isabel, on the other hand went from frightened lonely target to confidant strong woman who walked away unharmed and unafraid.

18. Sex and money

No, we are not going to talk about money for sex. Prostitution has little to do with sex. Those poor girls are submitting their bodies to unwanted sex with men they have no desire for, only to make their rent, send their kids to college, in some case to pay for a drug habit and often to avoid beatings from their cruel pimps. As to the users who keep this ugly trade alive and well, I wonder if they realise they are contributing to the misery of those modern day slaves. Enough said.

Within a real relationship or a marriage it is customary to pool your incomes together and budget. When one of you is down on his or her financial luck, the other will support him or her until he or she finds their financial feet again. That's fine. But that is the only situation when you can accept or give money to a man, especially a man you are dating, no matter if it is recent or not. A man whose intentions are good has no business asking a woman for money. It is quite normal and even lovely to receive or give presents to your lovers for birthdays or at Christmas, my shag buddies regularly bring me fine chocolates, French perfumes, scented candles, books or even sexy lingerie (Igor's specialty). Or you can pick up the check at the restaurant or the movies sometimes. That is so nice and pleasant for all concerned but this is as far as it can go with a sexfriend or a potential boyfriend.

Sex, it has been said, brings you money and power. Power to distract a potential trouble maker from hurting you by smiling in a way that makes him feel handsome? Sure. Power to sway a traffic warden off giving you a parking ticket because you bat your eyelids and unbutton your shirt enough to show some cleavage? Absolutely. It is only short lived but it works well into your forties.

However men have this power too and some of them use it against us for material gain. We all know of young gigolos selling their charms to rich old ladies. I am here to tell you that many young men are fascinated by older women and are very happy to bed us for free. A French man I interviewed on the subject told me that he prefers older women because *"they are confidant, experienced, financially independent, never have any plans to settle with me or force a pregnancy on me."* That seems to sum up what all younger men who sleep with older women think. Yay for mature women! We no longer have to pay for gigolos to swallow Viagra or snort coke to pretend to drill into our bodies with their eyes closed. We can have the real thing for free!

There is a dangerous kind of predator who cleverly spots vulnerable lonely innocent women who still believe in love. At first he will be friendly and charming enough to gain your trust, suddenly he will find himself in a difficult situation. "He owes his bookmaker a few hundred dollars in or else he will be severely beaten up and it will be your fault. He must pay a few thousands for his grandmother's surgery or else she will die in atrocious pain and it will be your fault. He is behind on his alimony, his ex wife is threatening to never let him near his kids again, how can you not help? Have you no heart?

His business just needs a financial boost to make it big, you could end up being the girlfriend of a future Donald Trump if you play your cards right! Does any of this sound vaguely familiar?

When conmen approach you they never ask you for money directly, not unless they are very, very untalented. They talk you into wanting to help, soon you are motivating yourself to part with your money because of something he hinted but did not actually say out loud. Which gives him plausible deniability. Because you think there is a bond between you, no written agreement was signed and you won't even be able to sue the conman when you discover there are no bookmakers, grandmothers, kids or firms. This can cost you a couple of hundreds to a couple of thousands. Sometimes the conman returns with a fake excuse, has sex with you, to bind you to him and sponge some more money off you! The more vulnerable the victim is, the more in denial she will be. Ladies, please don't let this happen to you anymore. It is best to be by yourself that to try to buy a predator's affection.

One night stands and sexfriends are there to fill our sex lives for free. There is no need to pay for sex.

Let me repeat this loud and clear for everyone to know: THERE IS NO NEED TO PAY FOR SEX !

We are women... we can always get laid for free and we don't have to be tall, young, blonds or skinny to get laid. This is one of our powers, we can always get laid for free and for real. Long live to one night stands, quickies, experiments and shag buddies! That's what there are there for. When you are the boss of your sexlife you identify conmen, thiefs, dominant tyrants, abusers and predators easily and just run away from them because you are no longer vulnerable to their emotional blackmail.

Their subliminal threat is:

"Do as I say, give as I want or else I won't love you and if I don't no one else will."

When you feel unsecure and lonely you would do anything to hold on to an illusion of companionship, but if you are the boss of your sexlife you will tell yourself:

"Who does the jerk think he is? If he won't give it to me I will get it elsewhere, let's go cruising tonight."

And on you move, with your heart and your bank account intact.

19. Fight sex with crazy Angelo

Angelo was a virile handsome Spaniard wine salesman in his mid thirties whom I met trough my best friend Caroline when she gave him a lift as we were running some errands in town. That morning I was looking less than presentable, unwashed hair, red nose and broken voice from a recent cold. How that had appeared attractive to Angelo, I will never know. I barely said hello to him when Caroline introduced us as he got inside the car, right behind her. We carried talking about our children and what we were cooking for dinner that evening; I hardly noticed it when she dropped him off. Imagine my surprise when Caroline rang later to ask if it was okay to give Angelo my number!

Who was Angelo? I had forgotten all about him. Curiosity got the better of me and I found myself accepting to have dinner with Angelo two days later. We had some great Greek food, an interesting conversation and I accepted to see him again. On the third date he gave me a kiss goodnight that made my head spin and this led to more dating and finally some really, really good sex. I thought Angelo might make a fine shag buddy but I wanted to take it slowly because at the time Caroline and I had only been friends for a few months and I was terrified of losing her. Caroline is the antithesis of me. Sweet, romantic, highly educated, and she has been married to the same man for a couple of decades. We agreed on politics, religion and how to raise children but we had fundamentally different ideas about love and sex. She still believes in love, I don't. She maintains sex belongs to a loving and stable relationship; I use it as a weapon and a tool to have fun. Back then I was already the boss of my sexlife but I was waiting for the right time to tell Caroline about my unusual sexual behaviour. That meant I was playing a part with an Angelo who was your typical Spanish macho man who thought his girl should be submissive, available and non opinionated (did he pick the wrong girl or what?).

My hidalgo decided when and where we should meet and when we should have sex. Everything had to be on Angelo's term. Twice, he wasted my time by calling me over and deciding that he wasn't in the mood so we would just talk instead, I was seething! The second time he displayed power, I slammed the door of his apartment. He rang later to say he didn't want to have sex with me, that he would never touch me again. Grrrr. Was that supposed to make me yearn for him?

He obviously didn't know who he was trying to tame and my reaction to his rejection was to jump in another man's arms, a gorgeous lawyer called Mickey, practically in front of him. I came out to Caroline about being the boss of my sexlife and guess what? She still loved me! My lifestyle was not for her but she tolerated it quite well. I had liked Angelo and I wanted to make him want me again so that I could negotiate our affair on my own terms this time. My subliminal message to him was to be:

"Don't you dare blackmail me sexually because I

can get laid anytime I want; I don't need your dick even if I like it. I can get any dicks anywhere anytime."

A few weeks later, Caroline and Jeff threw a huge party to celebrate a major promotion he had gotten. Angelo was there, so was I. He turned up with some bimbo he kept toying with, making sure they were always within a couple of feet from me. I had attended the party alone, as I always do. Angelo's games were a little unnerving and I had the impression that everyone was talking about us. That was until I spotted this classy very beautiful man who had women practically queuing up for him. Not only was he movie star handsome, he looked like one too. His natural elegance gave him an aura of irresistibility that drew anything female to his face. Sexy without even trying, hmmm my kind of man. My friend Caroline saw that I was interested and explained Mickey was a corporate lawyer who worked with Jeff and a nice person too. And he was single! I told her Mickey was way too hot to be a nice person, but I didn't mind because what I wanted did not require a long term commitment. Yes, Mickey would be my tool to get Angelo back.

"Oh but don't you want to patch things up with Angelo?" Caroline wondered.

"Nope, I replied, I just want to show him who the boss is."

I stood somewhere Mickey could see me and I just stared at him silently while he flirted with one girl after the other. I overheard him say that he would never date a woman who doesn't drink nor smoke because he would find it boring. Aha! A challenge! Intrigued by the stranger who was cheeky enough to look straight into his eyes and not lower her gaze when he looked back, Mickey came over to introduce himself to me, unaware that my friend had already given me all the details about who he was and what he did.

"Care for some champagne?" even his voice sent tingles to my toes! I politely declined and looked him straight in the eyes:

"I don't drink nor smoke and I find you very attractive, wanna dance?" He did. While we danced slowly we made small talk and I discreetly checked on what Angelo was doing. He was kissing his bimbo while looking right at me. Good, the reaction I was aiming for. Mickey was happy to follow me to the bathroom for a make out session; we walked there slowly, holding hands. And yes, we walked right past a fuming Angelo. Fortunately Mickey was a fantastic kisser and before things got out of hands, I said he was too good for something quick and sordid. Mickey was to drive me home and call me the next day. We exchanged our numbers and he went to the cloak room to get our coats. I stood by the bathroom door and pretended to reapply lipstick in my tiny evening purse mirror. I stayed there at least five minutes to make Angelo boil with jealousy at the thought of what he imagined I had been up to in the bathroom with Mickey. *Muahahahaha*! Childish, I know, but I had gotten what I wanted. Angelo wanted me and he was hardly looking at his unsuspecting bimbo anymore. A couple of days later I had a date with Mickey. First I had to endure the ritual of classical first date. Boring dinner and eluding a third degree. I was hoping this would be worth it and discreetly checked my watch as I wanted to get shagged, showered and safely back home in my pyjamas before the midnight movies started on television.

Yes, you read me right; I wanted to hurry that date in order to make the creepy movie on time. I'm a television junkie and I am proud of it. Also I had booked a sitter only until that time. Life is much simpler when it is organised. There is a time for everything. A time to eat fine food with friends or family, a time to date , a time to get wild and a time for crazy shagging with some hot stranger. There is a time to work hard and a time to relax in front of the TV with my purring cat, last but not least, there is a time to come home and pay the baby sitter before your kids know you were even out. With a modicum of organisation, you can have it all!

In the restaurant, most of the women present were looking at Mickey. The waitresses were smiling at him and the customers were ignoring their own dates. Ah the pros and cons of dating a strikingly beautiful man! Next time, I declared, we will skip dinner and jump straight into bed or bath tub or on the dining table. Whatever he fancied. He was just too hot to waste even a nanosecond of. Mickey was absolutely magnificent in bed! Such was his expertise that I forgot all about Angelo. One afternoon I was lying in Mickey's arms basquing in post sex beauty and the love making had been so wonderful that I found myself thinking: *This is it. This is it! Sex doesn't get better than that. I could die right now and have no regrets because I got to sleep with Mickey.* A million orgasms and other lovers later, I did change my mind, of course, but this is how I felt that morning with Mickey. I'm not easily impressed but that man really impressed me. We saw each other for a couple of years until I called it off one morning when I realised I was liking Mickey much more than I should be. I was feeling like socialising with him, I wanted non sexual quality time together. Dangerous feelings to have when you are the boss of your sexlife! When I identified the potential danger, I broke up with a stunned Mickey who didn't understand what I was talking about.

It would have been really hard work to make it last with an international lawyer who was constantly travelling all over the world, I wasn't prepared to keep my legs closed that long. Class difference took care of the rest. I guess lawyers and working class women don't mix well. Last but not least, there was also the small matter of Mickey never listening to a word I said – until I broke it off. He heard me then.

Let's go back to my little stunt a couple of years before that had worked on Angelo when I made him jealous at Caroline and Jeff's party. Soon Angelo was calling me, demanding if I had "done" Mickey. I toyed with his insecurities and just refused to answer, which drove my Spaniard crazy with doubts.

Our phone calls always sounded the same:

"Why won't you tell me?"

"Because that's none of your business Angelo. Why do you even ask?"

"Just curious, that's all. He is a *maricon* anyway (*gay in Spanish*), I'm sure nothing happened."

"Mickey is no *maricon*, I can assure you."

"How would you know? Did you do him?"

"None of your business, *cabron*!"

"Come on, you can tell me, I won't tell anyone. Maricon... right?"

"As man as you are, *pandejo*, now stop asking and go do some young bimbo."

"Yes or no, don't play with me, *joder* !

"*Cariño*, this is really for me to know and you to find out"

Angelo was fuming. The sparring in Spanglish was so much fun.

One evening, Caroline had had enough of this childishness and asked Angelo over for coffee and she also invited me. There was so much tension that it was palpable. Caroline tried to maintain a civilised adult conversation but Angelo and I started a word war, tearing each other apart while smiling diplomatically and complimenting my friend on her exquisite blue china coffee cups from Prague. At some point Caroline gave up on us and retired to her bedroom asking us to sort it out like grownups would. I went to the kitchen to make myself a sandwich. Angelo followed me and asked me again if I had made love to Mickey that night at the party.

I had already done so, post party and a few times too but I loved tormenting my macho Angelo. He opened the fridge to pick up a jar of mustard; I made a wrong move and bang! The jar was shattered on the kitchen floor.

"Hombre! look at what you made me do." he squealed.

I laughed at him. Angelo grabbed the glass of coke I was holding in my hand and spilled it over my chest.

What an idiot! I quickly bent down to dip my fingers in the mustard on the floor and smeared it all on his nice Armani shirt. He was furious! I started removing my shirt while complaining that I now had to go to the bathroom to clean that mess he made, when a very wild Angelo stopped me in my tracks grabbing me for a hard kiss that told me the whole arguing was seriously turning him on. I pretended I wanted none of it and pushed him conveniently on the couch. He immediately pulled me to him and we had wild, insane fabulous fight sex all night. We rocked around the living room, breaking a couple of lamps and making a general mess. We had violent intercourse; there was nothing sexy or cool about it. Angelo wanted me because I had questioned his alpha maleness and I wanted Angelo because he had said he would never touch me again. It was about power. We were empty, spent and breathless on the floor but there was none of the post orgasm glow normally felt at such times. I got up and lowered my partly torn skirt over my laddered stockings. The Spanish tiger on the carpet got hold of my left ankle wanting to know where I thought I was going. I fished my blouse out of a terrarium where a couple of sleepy turtles would have something to gossip about for centuries. My blouse was ruined; I shook my ankle free and put my jacket on. He realised I was leaving he raised himself on an elbow and cursed at me. What had I done, he asked sleepishly. What had I done? I told him. *Simply having sex with the man who coldly told me he would never touch me again, mi amor. And you can fix that mess we made too.* That felt so good to take back the power from this macho man.

The taxi driver hesitated letting me in; I looked messy and smelled funny. He probably had no idea why I was smiling to myself. Something tells me Angelo will think about it twice before pushing a girl's pride around.

20. Mehmet: Dealing with a psychopath

In 1991 I stayed in a hotel in Lugano for a couple of weeks. The cute Macedonian breakfast waiter was always flirting with me and I thought it innocent and amusing. I slightly flirted back but nothing happened because I was married to Jake at the time. Years later I walked into a sushi bar in Zurich and there he was again. Mehmet (name changed) was then divorced as was I, and when he hit on me I let nature take its course. It was a pleasant affair for a couple of months. We had a huge argument when I found out the supposedly divorced wife in Macedonia was not only still relevant but pregnant and on her way to Switzerland with all their three children. I was disgusted at the deception and wanted to break up. Why do married men lie about their status? How is one to know who is free and who is not?

Instead of calling him to say I was leaving because of his treachery I was stupid enough to actually go up to tell him face to face, thus walking into a trap.

Not a good idea, not a good idea at all.

You would think Mehmet would have been apologetic and ashamed. Well you would think wrong. The adulterer was quite arrogant about lying to me, to his wife and to a couple of others. Yes the creep was two timing everybody. During a very heated discussion I called Mehmet a liar and a cheater, expressing my regrets for his poor wife. How do you think he reacted when it finally downed on him that I was leaving? You will never guess in a million years.

"But you are a cheater too, he snarled, you have always cheated on me from day one! I have put up with you sleeping with another man for years, you have been cheating on me for years!"

For years? But I had only dated him for a couple of months, what years?

"What years? I demanded to know, you and I have only seen each other for a couple of months, how could I have been doing anything to you for years? I don't understand."

I really did not understand, I bet you don't either. The problem was, maniac Mehmet had counted the very first day we met, years ago, as the first day of our relationship".

"Are you joking? I cried with horror, I was married to Jake at the time and I never even touched you. I didn't even know your name. There was nothing between us at the time."

"Liar! he yelled, we had something going on in our hearts. You were always smiling at me and sleeping with Jake at the same time, you are a whore! You betrayed me with your husband!"

Speechless. I was speechless. Not a usual state for me to be in. I began to understand in how much trouble I was. Mehmet was a very disturbed man who had delusions about the pleasant customer who innocently smiled back at the breakfast table. And every time I spoke of my husband Mehmet took it as cheating. How could I have known? This couldn't be happening. I realised I was in danger when he picked up a bottle of beer in one hand, brutally pushed me down on his couch with his other hand, grabbing my throat to force me to stay down. He looked at me with cold hatred and quietly said:

"Shut up bitch, you are not going anywhere anymore."

Not good, not good.

While he was threatening me, his phone rang. He started flirting with some unsuspecting girl, still half choking me! The nerve of that mad man was astonishing. Accusing me of cheating with my own husband at a time I barely knew the lunatic and flirting on the phone with some girl right in front of me.

I was furious with myself. How could I have been so stupid to get involved with a dangerous psychopath and end up in such a horrible situation? The guy was obviously mentally ill and even if he would kill me tonight, his lawyer would get him off the hook because of whatever mental disorder causing his vicious actions. What worried me the most was how this would impact my teenage children, what would my family think if they heard that I got murdered in a grotty apartment by a crazed married Macedonian in the middle of the night? Could it be more embarrassing?

Out of sheer desperation, I had a stroke of genius. I smiled at my aggressor and whispered:

"Cheri, pour me a drink and give me a fuck."

Mehmet was so surprised by my most unexpected reaction that he released my throat immediately, shaking his head in disbelief.

"Since when do you drink?" The couple of seconds it took the psycho to process what I had just said was enough for me to jump off his couch, grab my purse off the floor, hurriedly unlock his door and literally fly down the staircase. I had almost reached the ground floor when Mehmet screamed from the top floor banister:

"Cherie! Where are you going?"

(*Where am I going? Away from you lunatic!*) I shouted back, without slowing down, that I was going to the corner shop to buy him cigarettes. If the man was really mentally ill, he wouldn't realise it was too late for shops to still be open. I can truly say I have never run faster in my entire life. While he kept ringing until I switched my phone off, I ran and ran. Adrenalin was raging all over my body while I ran nearly an hour to get back home. So scared was I, that I wouldn't even stop running to hail a cab or board a bus. Finally I got home noiselessly and locked myself in the bathroom. I was out of breath and sweating. I had a long shower. I felt so dirty. Why did I feel so dirty when I had been the victim? I kept scrubbing my skin until it was almost raw, my tears were flooding my face and I even had to throw up.

What had happened? I got myself into a potentially very dangerous situation with a sicko because I didn't notice the alarm signals and I forgot to be careful. How incredibly foolish of me! How did I get so lucky to get away intact? Did I even deserve this blessing? I was in turmoil, my head was spinning and my eyes were burning from all the crying. I threw up again and silently went to my bedroom to pick up pictures of Mehmet and I, hidden in my diary.

I went back to the bathroom, tore all his photos in tiny pieces and flushed them down the toilets. I mentally flushed him down the toilets too. Since I sustained no physical injuries, I chose not to report it to the police. They would have no case. What Mehmet did was unforgivable. Instead of saying he was sorry, he stalked me for months! Calling me every day, leaving hundreds of voice mails, waiting for me outside work, hooting from his car when I would ignore him.

My way to cope with this was to completely cut all ties with my stalker. I never returned his calls or texts. I never responded to his provocations. I never even confronted him about his attacking me. I totally erased him from my life and that really hurt him. He once left a voice mail saying that he was happy to at least hear my lovely voice on my answering service. I deleted it on the same day and replaced it with an electronic voice message. His next message was to plead to have my actual voice back on because he missed it. I refused to keep up the past connection and kept ignoring him; whenever he appeared I just walked away discreetly. Whenever he saw me with a man, I didn't do anything provocative but I was relieved that he saw me moving on with other guys. Had he not called me a whore once? I suppose that is what a free independent woman is, in his opinion. I took that as a compliment. Better be called a whore by a psychopath than being his submissive victim. This went on for months.

Fast forward a couple of years later, I was having a meal alone in some sushi bar when in came Mehmet. I didn't recognise him at first because I wasn't wearing my glasses. I just saw a cute guy smiling and walking towards me. As he sat near me and I got a closer look, I nearly jumped out of my skin. He told me not to be afraid, he had not thought of me in years and he was as surprised to see me as I was. Mehmet went on to apologising about attacking me that night a couple of years ago. Post traumatic stress from war with Serbia and alcoholism had driven him insane and unaccountable. That was his excuse for his aggressive behaviour.

He quickly added that he had stopped drinking for two years now, was with alcoholic anonymous and had a stable job. I quietly accepted his apologies and left after a handshake. During the next months I bumped into my ex stalker a few times. At the money automat in a bank, in front of a shop window I was admiring or at the tea room where I was waiting for Leila. Each time he said hello and asked me out, each time I politely refused. When Leila saw him leave that tea room she noticed he had been working out and looked really hot.

He may look hot but he is a deranged weirdo so it is not worth it. I mentioned to Leila who wanted to know why I had forgiven him if I still resented him. Just because I forgave it doesn't mean I'm prepared to put myself in that trap again, I explained. One afternoon I was queuing up by myself at the cinema when a couple of guys gently tapped me on the shoulder.

Hello you! They asked friendly, Is Mehmet here? This doesn't seem like his kind of movie.

His two younger brothers! How did they even recognised me, it had been years. And how odd that they wondered if he might be at this movie with me. Why would anyone think that?

I greeted them back and asked what they had been up to. It turned out they had immigrated to Sweden and were in Zurich on holidays. From what they were saying I got the impression they imagined I was still dating their brother. Why would they think that? What was going on here? Finally I asked how they recognised me after all these years and was astonished to hear they saw me earlier on the framed pictures of us that their brother kept in his apartment. What! Not to mention the small picture he carried in his wallet to this day.

What?!

In his sick mind Mehmet still thought we were an item and he had built a complex fantasy and actually had people believing his delusions. It was worse than I thought. Skipping the movie, I rang the lunatic to confront him with his obsession and this time I was smart enough to do it on the phone. I refused his offer to meet for a drink and demanded an explanation. Mehmet pleaded with me not to tell his brothers, he wouldn't bear them knowing the truth. But why? That's what I wanted to know.

"It's not really a lie, I know you still have feelings for me and we will be back together someday because we belong together, it is not a lie it is merely anticipating."

He truly was insane, unpredictable and dangerous. I yelled at him, he tried to make me feel guilty, when that failed he started threatening me, when that failed he tried to charm me, when that failed he was aggressive again.

Frightening how fast a man can turn into a monster when you want to leave him. I went through the whole routine of being followed, called constantly and superbly ignoring him, for a few more months until he got the message and started to pester someone else. When someone stalks you, it is neither passion nor love, it is domination and total disregards for your feelings. You say no and he hears yes maybe.

It is brutal and borderline sadistic, a stalker is not interested in what you say and what you want. Therefore I elected to cut out all contacts to stop feeding his delusions. If this doesn't work you can always get a great lawyer.

21. Men prefer bitches

In case you don't already know, men tend to like bitches better than nice girls, which explains why so many decent girls cannot find a good man. We are raised to wait for prince charming and start a family. Boys are raised to be adventurous and daring, they play cops and robbers, cowboys and Indians, they learn to recover quickly from bruising, they are told not to cry, they learn to get up and go. We play little mothers with our dollies; we learn to be caring and nurturing. Can you see a pattern here?

Boys are never raised to wait for the princess! That's why they never appreciate them. If you are really lucky you might meet a real man who does want a woman who possesses intelligence, integrity, kindness and warmth. Even in that case, a real man might have to kiss a lot of frogs before finding his princess.

Unless you are extremely lucky, the chances are if you are a nice girl... you will never find a nice man. Nice girls have a long history of continually meeting the wrong man for whom they will do anything and gain nothing but yet another broken heart and the time honoured question: *what have I done wrong this time*?

What nice girls do wrong each time is treating all their boyfriends as a potential husband. They show him their true personality and what great wives they would make. They give their man everything, love, compassion, emotional support, financial support.

They show their housekeeping skills and cook romantic meals. They completely involve him in every aspect of their lives and automatically give him exclusivity even when he doesn't ask for it. A man gets overwhelmed with all this sweetness at first and then he gets scared when he feels his freedom threatened, he moves on to the next unknown territory. That's all. The crying nice girl blames herself and refuses to give up on love, she nurses her bruised soul with the help of her girlfriends who have been trough the same time and time again. One day she goes looking for love again with a heart full of hope and she heads for another disaster. A nice girl is so desperate to find love that she gives away those desperate vibes that will attract predators. Liars, blackmailers, users, wife beaters, drug dealers, conmen and the scum of the earth spot those potential victims easily. Bad men will hurt those nice girls and that will make them more vulnerable to even worse men. They will part with their money, reject job opportunities, give up their friends and tolerate physical abuse just for the sake of having a man, in the delusion that they might change him into a real man.

Here is a scoop ladies: you cannot change a man, he has to want to change for himself.

A lot of men will live la *vida loca* until they get older and feel too tired to work hard at seducing new lovers and they will pick the current one to be their companion. Now that we have established why men do not love nice girls, how do they feel about bad girls?

The answer is they love bad girls. Bitches, selfish, self centred, cold, bad, bad girls, the worst the better.

But why? Simply because they can never be sure of a bad girl's love. They will work hard at trying to monopolise her attention, her affection and when she slips between their manly fingers their hunter's pride gets so offended that they need to try again until they win. But the bad girl refuses men's dominion and reclaims her freedom even when men pretend to make nice in order to conquer her wild heart.

When I was a nice girl I got screwed over so often I took a year off men to ponder my situation and my solution was to become the boss of my sexlife, which in men's words means: a bitch.

If I had a dollar for every time a man, realising that I was not allowing him to treat me like his toy, retaliated by calling me a *bitch, a salope or a Kurva...* I would drive a Porsche by now. Since I became what most men identify as a bad girl, meaning a non-victim, I get more attention, more respect and much, much more sex from them. Men have completely lost their power over me and it is a huge component of my happiness today. What men don't know is that I am in fact a nice girl. A very nice girl, romantic, kind, open, honest and warm, with so much love to give. If men knew this, they would eat me alive, but I make such a good job of concealing my inner nice girl that they imagine I'm a bitch and they eat in my hand instead.

22. Are real men sensitive and emotional?

Some discussions I have had recently with my daughter and with some friends have made me wonder about this. What if real men were actually fully equipped with a brain and a heart? What if real men were actually sensitive and emotional?

From the stone age all the way to the eighties and nineties, a man, an alpha male, a real man was by definition heartless, selfish, totally insensitive (except for football), narrow minded, chain smoking, heavy drinking, oblivious to beauty and somewhat ignorant. A man was traditionally tougher than us, more academically educated than us, less smart than us and didn't know a thing about cooking or healthy eating. He had to be straight (at least officially), homophobic, he was never involved in the education of his children and remained absolutely clueless about female orgasms, giving equally bad sex to his wife and mistresses while demanding complete obedience and fidelity from said poor wife and mistresses. He also expected his wife to abandon her career and stay home as soon as they were married. Does that remind you of anything?

Unfortunately, there are many countries that are still stagnating in this nonsense.

We in the free world have fought hard for our rights and as we got more and more freedom, our men have began to evolve beautifully.

Today's men are taking care of themselves, eating sensibly even quitting smoking or actually exercising because they want to look good. Today's men want to be desired by women. They enjoy being sexy and have women looking at them. They read books and learn about how to be better lovers; they know all about the G spot and how to stimulate what. The new real man doesn't just masturbate with your vagina before falling asleep, the new real man wants to see you come; he takes pride in giving you pleasure with his sexual skills. He is aware of his woman's needs. And when we tell him we are not yet ready to have children or that we are not his servants, he tries to charm us rather than impose on us like his forefathers did.

More and more men are involved in the raising of their children. I know a few who made the choice of becoming stay at home dads and love it. They don't even mind their woman being better qualified and on higher wages than they are. They share the household chores too.

By the time I was a young mother, in the late eighties, I was working fulltime. I would put in a nine hours day work and come home to my husband who had done the same but now expected to be served a fine home cooked meal in a spotless apartment. Like most European women of those decades I actually had to work twice without getting any credit for it. Men had stopped forbidding their wives to work but they still felt that a woman's work is less important than a man's. In Switzerland it is normal for a married woman to work but men are still better paid than women for exactly the same job and with the same qualifications. Not to mention the fact that working mothers are still being frowned upon when they have a husband.

There is still a lot of territory to win here, let's go back to what it was like around thirty years ago. My husband and I use to clash constantly about his caveman attitude and I so resented the lack of sharing chores that it affected my libido, especially when I was told that sex was his conjugal right!

Back then it was the norm, girls were educated on archaic principals such as it is up to the woman to keep the marriage going. Or good girls don't like sex or married women shouldn't work or even you are a spinster if you are not married by the age of twenty five and the classic children raising is a woman's matter, which gave men permission to do anything and anyone they wanted to, whilst denying us all those privileges. Nowadays most modern couple have worked it out brilliantly. I was invited recently to a Thanksgiving dinner at a friend's house and most of the delicious food, turkey, stuffing, new potatoes, ginger glazed carrots and more had been cooked by her husband and he was pleased to share a few cooking tips and receive compliments. My daughter has many talents but cannot cook to save her life, at the beginning of each new relationship she warns her boyfriends who always answer that it is ok because they cook quite well anyway. The only one who tried to force her to cook didn't last very long. So they cook, they help looking after the kids, they do their share of cleaning and laundry...what else do they do? They look nice for us. Real men look after their bodies. They take care of themselves; hygiene and grooming are no longer considered unmanly. Real men also enjoy being better lovers; they don't just hump and snore within ten minutes. They want us to scream their names and come all over the places; they want us to tell them how wonderful they made us feel with the things they were doing to us. They need to know that they are the best we ever had. A real man doesn't squash and frustrate his woman, a real man is proud of her accomplishments; he is pleased to know he chose well. He doesn't want a servant, he wants a partner. Ever watched a romantic comedy with a man? A real man? They might not shed a tear when Bridget Jones finally gets to kiss her man in the snow, awwwww, but they will complain if you abruptly change channel. If in front of other alpha males they will grunt and scratch and act like apes but once alone with you they will revert to loving teddy bear mode. Whilst we have had to toughen up and harden ourselves to survive with dignity in a men's world, a lot of men got in touch with their heart and are no longer afraid to open up or even to show their vulnerability to the woman they have conquered and not vanquished.

Why are new real men acting so sensibly? Could it be that they don't want to repeat the mistakes their fathers and grandfathers made? Do they want their women to have a better life than their mothers had? Or are real men those who have been raised singlehandedly by strong mothers and strong sisters like my son was? Who cares? Not saying all men are like this, my point is real men are.

Ladies, if your man treats you badly, pushes you around, never listens to a word you say and trashes your feelings. If your husband fucks you but never makes love to you, never bother to give you an orgasm or two. If your boyfriend cheats on you, lies to you, never helps around the house. If your guy often brings his mates home without a word of warning but never lets you invite your friends. If your man is brutal, ignorant, macho and selfish, then you don't have a real man... you are living with a caveman who thinks men have to behave like gorillas on acid.

23. If he says no, just let him go

Sometimes a man says no. There can be many reasons for his turning down a booty call. Is he religious, is he in love with someone and oblivious to other women, is he gay still in the closet? Could it be that he just doesn't like your appearance or the way you made a pass at him? Maybe he likes them younger, older, fatter, skinnier, smarter, less smart, complicated or easy. Who cares why he doesn't want to date you? The point is he said no.

Whatever the reason for his unfavourable reaction, take it with a smile and bow out graciously while you still possess all your dignity. Do you really want to hear why he doesn't want to get bouncy with you? The answer is, you do not. Rejection is very unpleasant to take but listening to reasons why you are being turned down would be even worse. I am no stranger to rejection myself, I haven't always gotten every single man I wanted either. But I loved myself enough not to waste another minute on someone who clearly was not into me. Why should I?

We all know how hateful it is when a man we politely turned down keeps pestering us again and again hoping that one day we will be too tired to fight back and actually give in. What do we think of such annoying jerks? That's right. Would you want any man to think of you that way? No.

The physiology of desire is complicated. It takes lots of chemical reactions starting from the brain to rush all this blood into to that little thing down there and turn it into a rock hard pleasure tool. It also takes work to maintain an erection for an hour or two. This can only take place if every fibre in that man's being absolutely wants to shag you. You cannot talk him into it or force him if he is not having a hard on for you naturally. When this happens, just walk away, and do it without insulting them because you would only despise a guy who calls you names when you say no. There are enough shaggable men in your city who will be more than happy to know you intimately.

A word of warning here. If you are in a relationship that is falling apart, you need to dry your tears and prepare for a new life post him. The worst thing you can do is getting pregnant against his wish.

First of all, your guy might not even stay with you and the child. Even if he does stay for the sake of the innocent child you are using as blackmail, he will resent you and sometimes hate the child who is unwillingly forcing him to stay with a woman he doesn't love anymore. Would you want to impose this on yourself and your innocent child? To those of you who think their man will change once he is married or once he is a father, I will answer NO. Men never change unless they really want to. There has to be a profound will to change and this cannot be forced on them. My own father was a young cultivated gay man in the closet for years. Himself an unwanted child like me, he had suffered a lot of beatings at the hands of his own father and could never be who he really was. So serious was he about remaining in the closet that he chose a brutal profession, army combat instructor, although he was highly educated and a very gifted painter. This fear of people finding out he was gay also lead him to marry a very brutal and mediocre female who didn't possess an iota of integrity or intelligence. Within a few years he tried to break free but she got herself pregnant to force him to be chained to that mockery of a marriage. As a result, my brother and I became battered children too, unwanted and unloved. We somehow manage to break free ourselves, in our thirties and we moved on to happy marriages, raising happy children, but we were extremely lucky to escape the vicious circle of hatred.

It wasn't easy; we needed years of therapy and constant soul searching. We had to overcome the terror of what we had been the victims of, in order to face our fear and vanquish it. We had to learn to love ourselves so that we could love our children and the people in our lives. All this pain could have been avoided if some stupid female had not imposed us innocent children on a man who had clearly said he never wanted any.

Not everybody is that lucky. Why am I exposing myself to you? Only so that you will know to walk away from a man who says no. No thank you. Not anymore. Never again. No.

Insisting to conquer or to keep a man who says no, only brings misery and pain, sometimes over a couple of generations. So please if he doesn't want you, walk away before a disaster happens. Let him go. There will be others who will want you.

24. Do not tell your new man all about you

We have all made that mistake from time to time, so most of you will know what I'm talking about. But how many of us realised it and actually learned from it?

This is never a problem with one night stands as there is not enough time to talk and much better things to do. It can be one with long term sexfriends, unless you make it a rule, like I do, not to give away any secrets or intimate details of your past. It always comes up within a real relationship and certainly is a must before getting married.

The new man in your life will at some point, hint, ask and finally demand to know everything about you. Your past, your exes, your pains, your troubles, who was mean to you, who did you wrong and how, what did you enjoy or hate, what secrets you keep. To me this is a violation of my privacy. Sharing my body with my current man is a pleasure, isn't it enough? No, to men it isn't. They want you to share your past, your intimacy and your thoughts. Sharing this with my current man would be a major intrusion of my privacy. If a man tries to put me through a third degree, that immediately turns me off. You might as well date an FBI agent or an Inland Revenue employee if you wish to be scrutinised and analysed. Whatever you confess to your man will more than likely pop up during heated arguments, so be careful there.

First of all, talk as little as possible about your exes.

Only the relevant long term exes should be mentioned. Men are happy to brag about having had trillions of sex partners but their inner caveman still want that nearly virginal uncharted territory. Are they afraid we will compare them to previous ones? Do they lack confidence? The point is they don't really want to know that you are as free and as expert in sex as they are.

Say as little as possible. I'm not advocating lying but I am strongly suggesting omitting! Men are naturally competitive so if they hear that you gave Fred anal sex and did bondage with Sam or used to wear red lace for Tommy, they will want you to give them anal, bondage and red lace too. Their position being, if she gave this to other men, she must give it to me too! Territory marked.

A small portion of men might even ban these from your sexlife out of fear that this will remind you of sex with Fred, Sam and Tommy. You might also want to leave out any lesbian lovers unless you want him to constantly pester you with questions and maybe a private show.

Do not tell him of places you had al fresco sex, unless you want a nasty glare each time you drive past those places. Never ever tell your man how fantastic an ex had been and how great he was at doing this and that. You wouldn't like it either if he glorified an ex of his that way.

In fact, a new relationship is turning over to a blank page. Do you really want to pollute it with irrelevant past people or do you want to write about new exciting discoveries? That's right.

Of course there are special conditions where you both need to tell all. If this is the man you are going to marry and possibly raise a couple of children, a dog and a mortgage with, you need to both be honest about any details that might affect your future children and your marriage. Any diseases, history of genetic illness of any kind needs to be cleared before getting seriously involved. Is one of you barren? What religion if any will you be practising? Food allergies, addictions, any special likes or strong dislikes as well as career plans have to be defined and who stays home and how long to raise the kids? Will you have dogs or cats, what centre of interest you both share, how important sex is to you, what about fidelity? All this needs to be dissected thoroughly before taking the big step of getting married. Now is the time to talk if you have a crazy stalker who could be a threat to your man, if you are in a witness protection program or have made some powerful enemies in your past. Also discuss which paedophile uncles to stay away from at all time and the real reasons why you are not inviting such and such relatives to your wedding. Most skeletons got to leave the closets.

If after clearing all this you guys are still in love and still willing to take on the huge challenge of marriage and marital sex, I can only say : Good luck to you both.

This kind of two way confession is extremely exhausting and is only worth going trough for one, maybe two men in your entire life. Otherwise, avoid it all together as it can cut deep.

I never told either of my husbands that I had been a battered child, but not because of distrust, both my ex husbands are good men with principles. I chose not to tell them because I consider the matter closed. When my husbands or any boyfriends looked at me, they saw whatever they saw but not "that poor girl whose parents use to beat up black and blue, boohoo."

Whatever they felt for me, at least it was never pity nor contempt. I refused to allow what my biological parents did to me affect my adult life or my relationships to others and I certainly do not need to recreate a further violent abusive person in my life.

Of course a lot of my partners have demanded to know if I had any secrets, most wanted to know my past. That was always an aberration to me and when I replied it was the present that mattered, who cared about the past, they always had the same reaction. They felt I didn't trust them enough to confide in them. Mistrust was an issue but what held me back was knowing that they would someday use it against me, in one way or another. Besides, talking about a painful past is excruciating, why go through this again? And with each new man?

If they love you they will respect your boundaries. If they force themselves into your past against your will, you know who you are dealing with.

Now, a word of warning.

Never, ever, tell your man if you have been the

victim of rape or a battering husband or abused by your parents or your previous boyfriends.

Never admit to that.

Why? There is a very deep, dark, part in every man that will be triggered by such a revelation. Unless your man is a saint, (what is the likelihood of that?), a man who knows you are "damaged goods" will automatically allow himself to not respect you anymore. After all why should he? No one else has! Sad but true. Most men will give into evil and further your nightmare if he knows you are victim material he will never consider you seriously again. At first he might feel like the knight in shining white armour rescuing the damsel in distress but sooner or later he will think he is too good for you, that you should be grateful that he is not abusing you too like others have done. And someday he might turn into an abuser himself.

Unless he knows already, do not tell him or at least tell him as little as possible. Even men who are themselves former victims of abuse will not feel sorry for you and will not spend the rest of their lives making you feel safe and loved. Some will still be in denial and some will reject you while the rest of them will label you as "abusable". If you are in this situation, you have already suffered enough, please don't get into a vicious circle and do not tell your man everything about you that he doesn't absolutely need to know.

25. Don't let childhood abuse ruin your love life

You might think that those successes come easy for me, I'm confidant, my job is fulfilling, I am blessed with brilliant children, great friends and I can seduce almost anyone I like without getting hurt in the process.

Before you get really annoyed with me, let me let you in on a little secret: those things were not handed to me on a silver tray. I had to work very hard for each blessing, each triumph.

When we were little, my big brother and I were regularly beat up by our evil biological mother and her manic husband. Not only were we their punch bags, they always told us we were stupid, empty, a waste of oxygen and that we would never amount to anything. Oh I forgot... we were so retarded that no one would ever love us as we, of course were incapable of having feelings. Add lack of proper schooling in the mix and you might have a slight idea of the dysfunctional parents Pierre and I managed to have survived.

As we grew into teenagers, we were borderline masochists and very violent. As young adults we were lucky enough to find the right spouses who showed us that we were worthy of loving. A little therapy, much faith and tons of soul searching and discipline lead to who I am today. My brother is strongly agnostic and I am a strong believer. Pierre and I put a stop to the vicious circle and all our children turned out to be stable, smart, confidant and happy thanks to our being decent parents to them.

My brother has had a strong and happy marriage for over 30 years, I was less good at marriage but at least Jake, my first husband and I have a genuine and strong friendship to this day.

My friends all say I'm caring and loyal and my children think I am capable, loving and protective without being imposing.

You see, it can be done.

You cannot cancel out a horror childhood but you can refuse to let it ruin your whole life because if you do, you will allow the abusers to keep abusing you, way over the boundaries of time.

Is that what you want?

I didn't think so.

I could have been traumatised for life and become a battered wife or a tormentor, I decided to kick ass and become... me!

So if I can do it so can you.

26. Igor, j'adore

Igor (name changed) was an experiment my shrink had suggested a few years ago. The experiment was for me to try on a new kind of man: a normal, almost boring, man. White, highly educated, good manners, really good job, a divorce and a custody battle, Igor had been hitting on me for months and fitted the profile. He would be the perfect candidate for my experiment. Surprisingly, sex with Igor was breathtakingly fabulous. The man was very well endowed, loved foreplay and seemed to hear my thoughts at the right moments. We enjoyed a really pleasurable sex friendship during a number of months until one day he lied to cancel a date.

At least I think he lied since most men lie to us anyway – perhaps not all men but most of them. I was furious and broke up with Igor on the spot. I found comfort in the arms of my Nigerian shag buddy for a while but I was still a little upset. The very next day, Igor apologised profusely and asked to see me on the next day...only to cancel our date again with another lie! I had enough and never took his calls after that. Nice normal man indeed! I declared the experiment a failure and went back to dating bad boys. By the time Igor rang again, very apologetically, I had forgotten all about him and I politely turned him down.

A few months later a humbled Igor turned up at the centre where I work, handed me a beautiful bouquet of big yellow roses in front of everyone. I was touched by the romantic gesture, especially coming from a swiss man. They don't really like public display of affection. I gave him a thank you kiss and he walked away without saying a word. I looked around at my colleagues and they all pretended not to have noticed anything. Ahh! Swiss discretion. I felt sooooo horny, that the following Saturday I rang him and he practically sprinted to my place. Two hours of pure madness! Igor gives it really wild and dirty but also cuddly and romantic at the same time: absolutely magical. My body still ached from his and I wasn't able to even think about sex for a couple of days after that. I felt so high on the multi orgasms he gave me while Spain was victoriously kicking into European football championship. I missed soccer that night but we could hear Spanish people cheering loudly on the streets all over town. Igor giggled that we sure celebrated Spain going into the half final. After a couple of hours of giving me everything a lover can give the woman he has been desiring for months, Igor was locking me in his arms for some gentle post sex cuddling. I needed to know why he had insisted to get back into my pants and apologized as much as he had.

My hot Swiss lover revealed that he needed closure because he felt bad about the way we had left things. His divorce and custody battle were finalised, he had graduated from some super master degree he had taken, he had had a small tumour removed from his forehead and he felt the only unfinished business in his life was... me. He wanted forgiveness from disappointed me. He got it. He wanted this out of the way before trekking through India the very next week. I was impressed.

Then the sensitive, caring, considerate Igor morphed into a jerk, asking if I had a boyfriend.

If I had a what?

"Dude! I have just given you my body, would I have done that if I had my own man? Besides don't you remember I don't want one?"

It turns out Igor did have a serious girlfriend since a year. Great post sex conversation, isn't it? Picture this: the two of us are covered in sweat and body fluids, entangled into each other. Pulses racing, hearts throbbing, my body was still aching from his penis and his hands. His body was still warm from mine. The candles were burning, and lots of condoms were all over the floor. Spanish soccer fans were yelling their joy on the streets of Zurich and I could not believe what had just been said.

The idiot described how great that woman is and how his sons had already accepted her. In fact it was so serious that Igor was considering asking her to move in when he'd return from India. He was no longer in love like at the beginning but now it was getting serious.

Let's see if I understand how this works. One gets serious with lovers when they are no longer in love? Apparently one cheats on the girl they consider to be the one? How despicable! I am so glad to be single when I hear such things.

Now, was Igor doing this with the sole purpose of trying to hurt my feelings? Was he hoping to see me get upset and out of control, yelling, throwing him out maybe? Well in that case he wasted lots of time and energy for nothing. I remained ladylike, did my best not to vomit, and calmly asked about trekking in India. Small talks was all the reaction he got from me until he left, promising to call me upon his return in a month, if he wasn't too much in love. What?

I sincerely hoped Igor was just making the whole thing up just to freak me out because he knows I don't believe in cheating. You see, that is exactly why I don't like talking to the people I sleep with.

Liars... Cheaters.

Had Igor pulled this crap with a girl who didn't have my maturity and my knowledge, he would have caused some serious damages. I actually had no regrets, I had needed to get laid big time and I didn't get emotional about it. If that woman Igor is seeing, found out about me, who do you think she would blame: her liar or me?

One month later, Igor came back from India and jumped on his phone. He had been missing me. Or should I say: his body had missed mine. The newly returned Igor gave me multi orgasmic sex and kissed me all over. His desire for me was undeniable. And just as I had suspected, he had lied about having a girlfriend.

We are still sleeping together to this day. I never listen when he talks about his life and I never question. He is smart enough not to ask anything about my life. Pleasure with no strings attached, well under control. Maybe it wasn't revenge sex that night before India, or could he have been impressed by my classy attitude? I guess I was the best sex Igor ever had. Who cares as long as it works out?

27. The power of quickies

One morning I was doing my laundry while reading a book and baking some muffins, multitasking as usual. I was dreading a dental appointment that same afternoon and had again forgotten to reserve a bio turkey for the upcoming Christmas family dinner, to make things even brighter I was way behind on a ton of paper work. The phone rang at eight in the morning. There was Igor, seductively purring in my ears.

"Gut morgen shatzie (*Good morning, honey*)"

"Hmm, I grunted, hey you."

"I was just thinking of you after driving my sons to school and it is such a beautiful snowy day that I was wondering if you...."

"Sorry Igor, I bluntly said, I'm not really in the mood today. I don't feel sexy, I'm going to the dentist this afternoon, I have lots to do, books to read, stuff to file, my back is a little achy, my hair is not washed and I haven't even had my breakfast yet. So thanks for thinking of me but no thank you." I moaned grumpily.

"Hey, wanna a quickie?" he purred in a very intimate low voice that sent tingles to my toes.

"What?"

"I've got this massive hard on with your name on it. You fancy a quickie?"

All my stress and worries took second place to the

prospect of a quickie with Igor.

"Now you are talking! I smiled. Come on up, I feel better already."

Don't I always say that Igor is the perfect fuckbuddie in every way? No time wasting, lies or games, straight to the point, he knows what I want and what I don't.

How do you feel about morning sex? I just loooove it. When you are single you don't often get treated to it. It had been so long I almost forgot how fantastic a morning quickie could feel.

Igor comes in, unshaved, with his breath shallow and his mouth slightly opened. He pushes me against my front door after kicking it shut and begins undressing me feverishly while kissing me hard. His desire is out of control and really turns me on.

In such cases you either fall on the floor with your clothes around your ankles or if you are lucky you might actually stumble on the couch or the bed. Whichever comes first. But my morning stud is already inside my body before I'm naked and we are still standing against my front door. How clever of me to have carried a condom in my shirt pocket. Igor and I are against the door, my legs wrapped around his hips. Wouldn't it be hilarious if some Jehovah's witnesses just knocked on the door right now?

My naked thighs enjoy the feel of his jeans, the zip of his black leather jacket rubbing sensuously against my almost exposed breasts. This leather smell is driving me so wild with desire that I don't even mind the wall digging roughly in my back. My fingers are running frantically trough his dark blond curls and I can't stop feeling small waves of fire washing over me. Igor is practically dancing in my body as deeply as his tongue is doing tango with mine, yum. Since I'm smaller than he is, Igor has lifted me a little and is cupping my buttocks to secure me in that position. And what a position it is!!!

I feel so alive and sexy when he stares at me with half closed eyes and whispers:

"I love your ass...I love your tight mushi holding me so tight...I could kiss your tits all day...hmm I love your mouth...I love your eyes... (*My eyes? I thought we were talking about sex?*) I love to watch you come (*aha now I get it*)... I loooove to watch you come... come for me... come with me... come with meeeeeeeeeeeeeeee."

We rock into each other slowly, ever so slowly till we explode...

Later on we are sitting on the floor wordlessly, exhausted but happy. My head is resting on his broad shoulder while his arms and legs are wrapped around me.

He won't even shower, says he wants to keep my taste all day during business meetings and talking to clients, having a small reminder of this glorious morning. How is that for a sexy statement?

One more languid kiss and Igor goes back to his day. I found myself so energised by this fabulous quickie that I'm ready to take on the world! Roll on laundries, books, tax forms, gift wrappings and time tables; I'm ready for you now.

A quickie with Igor seems like the perfect way to start a long day. I know it sounds naughty but hey! I'm single. Therefore I am the boss of..... my.... what? That's right.

You might argue that having a boyfriend or a husband gives you access to morning sex as much as you want but, if your guy wants it in the morning, are you really going to take the time to have it? Will you be in the mood and forego your morning chores? And even if you do, will he bother to turn you on and make an effort to be sexy, to drive you crazy? Not unless you are very lucky. Most men take sex for granted in a relationship and stop making efforts to turn us on. This is what starts to make sex less and less appealing as time goes by.

Do you think Igor would have come up with this seductive call, this bad boy look and this brilliant wall sex in the morning, if he knew he could have me all the time at any time he wished?

That's right, I didn't think so either.

28. Separating sex from real life

One afternoon, as I was waiting for the green light to cross over, I saw some giggling school children who looked adorable. I looked up at whoever their dad might be and immediately looked away while turning bright red. That busy working single dad, holding his little boy's hand with one, a briefcase in the other, while shouting at his other little boy not to cross the road just yet and carrying a back pack full of groceries was no other that my volcanic red hot sex bomb Igor !

I was not at all expecting to see Igor in my neighbourhood at lunch time. I looked tired and messy after a shift of work, a half hour of jogging, carrying a bag of groceries and dressed in unflattering winter sport clothes. Oh no! If Igor saw me like this, could it be more off turning? The stupid traffic light insisted on remaining red and I couldn't help risking another look at Igor... Oh no! He was staring at me too!

My heart was racing as I pretended not to have recognised my favourite sexfriend. It occurred to me that Igor has already seen me exhausted, naked and dishevelled, even half asleep or barely awake. So, what was I hiding from? If my face kept blushing I was going to turn into a strawberry. Annoyingly, I couldn't help having fabulous shag flashbacks of the two of us melting into each other so profoundly only two Saturdays ago and how deliciously kinky Igor can get. This made me feel so turned on I was almost afraid to look at him again. I was having a strong inner debate at the traffic lights.

This is a moment in my real life, I argued with myself, there is a time for everything, I'm not in sex-mode right now and it is inconvenient to be distracted like this. Right now is time to be serious and bring my groceries home and get changed before going back to work doing some admin and preparing sessions and meetings. I cannot be on fire right now. Not now! Men are too much of a distraction if you take them seriously.

Finally the lights went green and I could cross over, away from my distractive sexy caveman, I thought it safe to turn back to take another look at that walking volcano.

Oh dear! Igor was still staring at me from a distance while tying one of his son's shoe laces. Was he pondering what I was pondering? Was his heart throbbing and his pulse racing like mine was? Was he having a mental argument with his dick? Not now! "Don't be such a school girl, I told myself. Don't get distracted."

It felt like two worlds colliding.

I strongly believe in compartmentalising every aspect of my life, the way you would separate different files from each other. And I need those files to never mix; I can't deal with them if they do. Silly? Probably but this is how I function. I do separate each aspect of my life methodically. I separate my job from my social life. I separate my spirituality from my sexuality. My sport training habits have nothing to do with my shopping behaviour or my dedication to reading. My family is my top priority before anything else on top of my priorities pyramid. My friends have no idea who my lovers are and my lovers have no clues as to who I really am and what I do. It would be confusing to me if an ex lover of mine dated a friend of mine, played golf with my brother, or ate at the same restaurant I eat with my actual friends.

That is the way it works for me, giving me total control over my life. Obviously, I cannot control everything, like health issues or the job market. But I can at least control my social life and have a *carpe diem* attitude while refusing men's dominion. My best friend said that it is a little paranoid, an ex-lover once called me selfish, most of others called me a bitch for it. What they call selfishness, I call self protection.

It would be impossible to separate all aspects of my life if I had a real relationship because men ask too many questions. When we ask our men questions, it is called "nagging". When they do it, it is called "being interested in what we do". I don't like being put through a third degree by my shagbuddies and in return I afford them the same courtesy. This can really upset men sometimes, a few guys complained that I don't ask questions because I don't care, only one clever French man once understood that I don't ask questions as a way out of having to answer any. What they think is lack of caring is simply respecting their privacy and... a diplomatic way to keep out of each other's real life.

What can possibly be wrong with that? Why don't they appreciate it? Or... could it be that they understand what it really means to me and are not happy to be on the receiving end of such behaviour?

There we have it, my secret to being happy and the boss of my sexlife is:

- No man in power position.

- Separate each aspect of your life.

Do you think I'm overdoing it ?

Would this work for everyone? Not sure, given the standards that are hammered into our heads since childhood, but it sure works for me.

29. The hypocrisy of open relationships

When I was married or in a serious relationship, I considered fidelity came with the territory of officially belonging with the man I loved.

Since I decided to remain single a few years ago and claim my sexual freedom, I simply refused any offer to get involved with anyone ever again. Besides the fact that a man would be unhappy with who I am now, I want to keep my options open to sleep around with whomever I wish, whenever I wish, but not at the cost of hurting someone's feelings. Although I am still a caring, nurturing, kind and loving woman, I just cannot put myself trough the whole charade again, giving one man an open invitation to violate my trust and trash my feelings at will. Never again. I also refuse the servitude of marriage that involves constant compromises, seeking or pretending to seek his approval and all this nonsense. If you are prepared to do this, do it. But if you are into your freedom like I am, just say no.

Hence my behaviour, I am no one's wife or girlfriend therefore I can do as I please without cheating on anyone. No partner gets hurt because of my frolicking with other single men.

My conscience is at peace.

I do know however four couples, one of them gay and two of them married, who practice open relationships.

People say, and I tend to agree, that an open relationship is only an excuse to cheat without any consequences.

Of course anything goes between two consenting adults, but are they really all consenting to their men or women having sex with others? How much of this is based on fear of losing their partner and intimidation that they must be extremely tolerant if they want to still be relevant?

Openly getting it on with others is better than lying, deceiving and cheating but I can't help wondering if the cheeky really doesn't mind? Not even a little?

A mate of mine once asked me to have sex with her husband in an effort to rekindle his failing interest in physical pleasure. (I kid you not). Her master plan was to walk in on us, pretended to be turned on and join in, eventually taking over. I politely declined after pointing out all the flaws in her brainwave.

What if he doesn't want you to join in? What if he really likes me or I really like him? Won't he feel a little angry/ disgusted/ used/ turned off?

Do you think she understood or should I have gotten more graphic?

Another time, this really attractive librarian once suggested she would make love to me while her husband watches. "It's ok, he doesn't mind." Oh, but I did!

Two of my shag buddies have asked me to threesome with them and another girl... they went very quiet and never brought it up again after I silently glared at them.

I have nothing against a threesome, I even had a couple of them in the past, but that was my decision, my curiosity and I had the power. But when a man organise a threesome and manipulates you into it, he has the power. He, not you. While I perfectly understand why some husbands require a threesome of their wives as a birthday present: they are getting older, bored and they get a kick out of doing someone else in front of their wives who has no right to complain. I get that, although I would never give a man of mine such a present. What is wrong with a gourmet dinner or a designer tie anyway?

Don't you find it a little creepy to have your husband sneak out to shag that gorgeous new waitress at the coffee house? Imagine a friend asking you what your plans are for tonight and you answering casually that you are watching the "Lord of the ring" trilogy while your other half is off to do this beautiful dentist but it is fine because you gave him permission to do it, besides it is only sexual and it won't mean a thing ?

"It is not cheating if we both agree."

Guys please! Are you serious? Get a reality check already.

I recently read an article in a famous lady magazine about a woman who had agreed to an open relationship in order not to lose her husband. It could not have been more pathetic. She had a whole list of does and don'ts for him to apply while screwing around with other women. Unrealistic rules such as:

He can't know their names, can't exchange numbers or emails, can't have the same girl twice, can't French kiss them, can give them head, can't gaze into their eyes and.

What was next? He is not allowed to come? How realistic is that?

I'd like you to visualise such a scene... two people are having sex, for no other reason that they feel like it and are attracted to each other at that moment. There is a lot of moaning, sweating, breathless panting going on. They are clearly enjoying themselves but they have to bear in mind, the whole time, that there are rules attached to this wonderful moment, they faithfully remember not to lock onto each other, not to kiss, they are not getting carried away at all.

What would they say to each other? When their mouths are not too busy to talk.

"Oops I've just French kissed you passionately; dang I shouldn't have done that! I feel ever so guilty..." She would say, and he would calmly reply:

"Tss, tss, tss, control yourself my dear... I would ask your name to shout it when I come but I'm not allowed." Her answer would be: "It's perfectly understandable, I really would not want to disrespect your wife, would I." And later: "'Scuse me, would you mind not twirling your tongue down there? I promised my husband I'd only do this with him."

His reaction would be: "Oh dear! I hope I wasn't

being too straightforward, I didn't mean to."

Oh yeah...! That will happen.

I used to quite like Karim, one of my favourite shag buddies until he asked me would I have a real and monogamous relationship with him. At some point I almost offered him an open relationship, he had never heard of it so I explained and he was so horrified that I wondered what had possessed me to offer him this in the first place. So I broke up instead.

There you go, lesson learned.

When I was a teenager, I read "Les liaisons dangereuses" and used to think it would be really cool to have a boyfriend like Valmont with whom I could be really naughty and adventurous, sharing experiences and comparing notes on it. When I did meet such a man, I realised it was not cool at all, at least not for me.

There you go, lesson learned.

There was this really gorgeous one night stand with whom I had kept in contact, against my better judgement. Out of the blue he told me he wanted to come down for a weekend, I was quite happy at the prospect of a shag fest with that hottie until he texted me to please organize a girlfriend of mine to threesome with us!

My disappointment was huge. I felt silly thinking that he had wanted to see me again just for me. Then I came to the conclusion that there was nothing wrong with me, he was a pervert macho who thought he could order me around. Well, not only my friends are not there to be abused, but I refuse to do something against my will.

He cancelled his trip and that was it. Had I been weak enough to grant the creep his wish, I would have been miserable to have given in, the said friend would never have trusted me again and the guy would still have walked out of my life after getting what he wanted. Might as well not give them the satisfaction.

There you go, lesson learned again.

If you fancy a threesome or an open relationship because you like it, then fine. But don't let a man force you into it. If he threatens to divorce or leave, you will be better off letting go of this domestic tyrant. Sex is the only time where we are truly free, totally attuned to ourselves and to nature, sometimes even to our lovers and to life itself. The very time where we have no fear is the time where we should have no restrictions either. To temper with this beautiful "me" time seems plain wrong to me, not to mention manipulative and unnatural.

What is it with guys and open relationships, porn and threesomes anyway?

If you have no desire left for each other, why don't you settle down for a loving friendship instead, like my ex husbands and I have? This is a really wonderful connection that cannot be messed up.

What say you?

30. Volker, the hot East German drama queen

One day of September 2010, I was at work one beautiful fall afternoon when I got a couple of saucy text from my favourite shag buddy Igor about how he would love to push me against a wall and... and... and... But he can't because he has his son this weekend. *Why did the plonker flirt with me then?*

Nuff said, not going to happen tonight.

But now I'm on fire after having reread the explicit details of what Igor is dreaming of doing to my body. I'm on fire, I'm on fire; what shall I do? Shall I call Mark who really wants to get back into my pants? Nah! Too soon. Shall I answer Karim's dozens of calls? Nah! Too clingy.

I know... I want something new!

In walks this really tall skinny white man, perusing at different products on display. I had noticed him before even though he was not really my style, but he was something new.

Let's take a closer look at this potential lover... he has got dark dreamy eyes, a cute twisted shag-me smile, long legs, wide hands with long fingers, six damaged fingernails, slight scoliosis of his upper back, flat feet. That will do fine.

I went over and chatted him up, I noticed he wore an electrician uniform, but sounded quite educated, probably German too. Volker (name changed) was soft spoken and good mannered, which makes me wonder if this hottie might be gay or bisexual.

He looked to be in his mid thirties and was shocked to hear I was soon going to be 50 years old within a couple of months. I always get that out of the way on the first contact, in order to attract only the men who like mature women. If they don't, they can always walk away and there will be no harm done.

I also was very clear that should something happen between us it will be physical only, because I really don't want a relationship, not ever. He replied he didn't want one either. Perfect!

Volker said he loves movies and wondered if perhaps we might watch a DVD at my place tonight?

Oh yes I'd love to "watch a movie" with you, (*you hot young thing*).

Since he was making eyes at me and talking in a Falco-like voice I mentioned casually he might want to call me sometimes....Volker said he would if he had my number. Oops I forgot.

I quickly jotted my number down and handed it to him with a cheeky grin....till he asked if it would be too forward to have my name as well? Oops I forgot again!

I was beginning to feel as awkward as a teenage girl with a crush. I held my hand out whilst introducing myself and he... kissed my hand! It had been a while since someone had kissed my hand in public and I blushed exceedingly.

I turned around so that he couldn't see my red face and uttered he should leave now because I had work to do and he... kissed my hand again.

Does that man like to kiss? How much of a good kisser is he? That's what I love about seducing someone new; the anticipating is such a turn on!

Volker rang on the very same night, out of the blue, to say that he was in my neighbourhood and wanted my house number. Quick! Within ten minutes I showered, got changed, tidied up my living room, fed my cat, brushed my teeth, hid my plate of spaghettis in the fridge and opened the door looking quite confidant to a smiling Volker who had no ideas of the marathon he had just provoked.

I made some coffee as we talked, I wondered why he followed me to the kitchen but I didn't let it throw me off my target. As I suspected Volker is German. He is actually East German, oh man!

Worse even he is not 35 at all, he is 29 years old! 29 years old for crying out loud! I told him he is twenty years younger than me,

I am twenty years older than he is, this can't happen.

This did not put him off at all, "how much of an issue is it really?" he asked. I thought about it for a minute and decided it was not. It is only going to be sex and no one will ever know anyway. So who cares?

At first we made a lot of small talk, I put on a DVD while he went on the balcony to smoke. I soon joined him and we stared at each other silently for a while.

"This would be the perfect time to kiss", I whispered and then Volker kissed me.

Oh what a kiss!

We kissed and kissed and kissed on my balcony. I wonder if my idiotic voyeuristic neighbour across the street was watching and pulled my new catch back inside my apartment. Volker kept kissing me as we fell on the bed, I told him we need to use condoms and he produced a whole box from his pocket.

At last, a clever boy!

So... we are in bed, everything is wonderful... there is a lot of touching and kissing going on... more kissing and cuddling... ok but now I want more so I go a couple of steps further and treat him to a fantastic blow job that he loved so much he... came.

Oh disappointment! Oh despair!

I pretended not to be annoyed and made out some more while he responded with tons of necking, petting and orgasmic kissing.

In spite of all this fairytale kissing Volker did not achieve wood, did not even make silly excuses, he simply commented on how bloody inconvenient that was. That's all, just "bloody inconvenient".

Still the whole thing felt as if we were making love, all the components were there, he was holding me, cupping my face, kissing me all over, looking into my eyes, moaning, whispering sweet nothings into my ears, he was so sensuous, loved being touched and voicing what he was feeling.

This is so sexy to me.

So we are spooning, groping at each other and the situation is still not getting harder. It was so beautiful that I decided that it didn't matter if he couldn't get an erection. Volker was so good at everything else that I was going to enjoy this weird non coital love making.

We carried on making gentle love like this for about two hours.

"You are insatiable" he gasped.

"I am, when something is so wonderful" I purred.

I wish more men would remember to cuddle during sex, like Volker does, or maybe they don't bother because they are too busy pounding away to remember tenderness and sensuality.

I don't know what is best: crazy humping or the long pleasure of making love without wood. Hmmm you know what that means don't you?

I am just going to have to keep dating lots of different guys who do it different ways in order to compare style and decide what I like best.

Yum.

On a funny note, I discovered, just on time, a text from my daughter that said she was on her way to sleep here after a concert. I diplomatically asked Volker to leave, he still took his time to shower and dress but he did leave on time after kissing me a million times more. Mmmmmm!

By the time my daughter arrived I had just finished

airing the room, changing the bedding, washing my hair, showering and changing into boring flannel pyjamas.

That was the most romantic date in the history of romantic dates. I hereby declared Volker welcome to watch movies with me at any time.

I dated him for a couple of months, each encounter more delicious than the other.

He had such a sexy charming careless way, calling in the middle of the night, texting at midnight to ask if I were awake or bored. On one such night I texted back that he could come in half an hour, he wanted to make that twenty minutes. I was looking forward to his magical kissing expertise.

That night the magic had taken a day off.

As soon as Volker arrived he jumped on me, so *unvolkerlike*. He was on fire and soon we were making out heavily on my couch, soon after that we were frolicking happily on my bed. aaahhhhh!

Guess who got wood this time? Yes!

Did he take Viagra? Did he snort coke? Do I care? I have no idea how he managed but the results spoke volume. Of course that sex was not Igor good or black men good but *Volkerwise,* this was really great.

Is it because he got more sexual that his kisses were far less magical?

Could it be my imagination? On the same morning I had seen this really romantic video of Seal and his wife, I guessed I wanted to recreate this atmosphere.

Not toniiiiiiiiiiiiiiiiiiiiight !

At some point in between kisses and caresses my eastern lover moaned some nonsense about being a bad man (No! really? I hadn't seen one for real before) and he plunged on my neck to bite me!

Ouch! That hurt. Man did I scream! I really don't know why movies always show women in ecstasy when a cute vampire bite them, that crap actually hurts. All he had to say in his defence was:

"See? I told you I'm a bad man."

Bitch please! Stop talking, stop biting and do me already.

My cat had seen Volker bite me and as he tried to kiss her goodnight before leaving she kept moving her little head away from his face. Ha! Ha! Ha! Ha! What a cool lady my cat is.

On another fabulous Saturday night he was practically sleeping after three orgasms, I had a caring gesture that I perhaps shouldn't have had; I covered him up with a blanket. He jumped up saying he wasn't going to sleep here (*fine by me*) because he wants to sleep late on Sunday mornings. Fine, I said, I need to get up at 8 am tomorrow anyway.

"Are you working tomorrow then?" he asked.

"No I never work on Sundays." I replied

"Why are you getting up so early then?"

"Because I want to go to Church."

"Where?"

"To Church!"

"You are actually a believer? A Church goer and all that?"

"Yeah I am, and?"

"But you can't go to Church tomorrow!"

"Why not?"

"You have made love tonight!"

Is that what it was? I giggled. "I made love, I corrected, I didn't kill anybody or broke the law, did I? I'm single and I can get laid as much as I want, I didn't even cheat on somebody."

"Why are you getting angry?"

"Who is getting angry?"

What a plonker! First he bites my poor little neck and now he questions my Christianity!

I distracted him with kisses and sent him on his way. He noticed a picture of President Obama on my pin wall and said: "Is that a picture of Obama?"

That kid sure can state the obvious, cant he? Yes, and? Some more kisses to get rid of him and he was fun again but he did warn me jokingly that he might become addictive for me.

Bitch please! I date black men, Latinos and eastern Europeans, among other things, men who get a long lasting erection on just a smile and they don't bite either. What made Volker think someone like me would be addicted to him? Can I not be nice to a guy without boosting his ego?

A dear friend of mine told me today that I tend to make my men feel good not just physically but emotionally too... Must be an extension of my work taking care of people. Now what was I going to do about those teeth marks on my neck?

A few days later I hit the sheet with my favourite sex friend Igor again, Igor is all about raw sex. He rips his clothes off, throws me on the couch, kisses me hard and gets down and dirty.

I love it.

But the day before I felt like calling Volker and he came running. I hadn't seen him in a while so that felt as something new!

I actually had butterflies in my stomach waiting for Volker. I treated myself to a facial and a long bubble bath, enjoying that butterfly thing. When he rang the door I checked myself in the mirror and saw that I still had some bits of facial cream on my neck! Yuck. Fortunately I live on the third floor and by the time my Easter promise got to my door the misshaps had been wiped clean.

Volker is the opposite of Igor. First he greets my cat properly and then we will kiss and make out for ages with our clothes on. It feels like when you are a teenager and won't go all the way with your boyfriend because you want to reach your wedding night still a virgin, putting all your sensuality in your kissing.

Oh what a fabulous kisser! He really takes his time to brush my lips gently, kiss me romantically, cup my face in his long slim hands, he caresses my legs, he stares right at me, he whispers.

His kisses are not foreplay kisses or even sex kisses, his kisses are orgasmic!

I love it too.

Last night Volker treated me to some serious romance. It was all about me. He managed some wood and I can't recall how often I came.

Even so it wasn't Igor's crazy pounding, it was tender and gentle and soft and warm and romantic. Volker kept gazing into my eyes and whispering how beautiful this felt. It was mind blowing.

I love men who voice their pleasure, Igor screams, Volker moans.

It was so magical I wanted to at least give him a nice blow job to show my appreciation. I had planted a few little kisses on his tummy when he pulled me back to face level and bang! There I was, under him. He wouldn't let me make love to him; he was quite happy making love to me and expected nothing in return.

This is the first time in history a man does this for me. What an incredible gift he gave me. I'm not saying I'd want this all the time but that night, I felt like a queen being so sexily pampered.

At some point Volker was resting on top of me. I laid there enjoying how nice this was, that big body on mine, his heart thumping hard on my chest, his head nestling in my shoulder, his hands still holding mine.

Don't you just love those moments when you are

both exhausted but happy, empty but energised, looking at each other without talking, basquing in the beauty of what you just gave each other.

Volker looked at me, pulled me to his chest and off we went on a magic carpet of creative body exploring.

Two beautiful hours later, he was resisting the temptation of sleeping in my arms and jumped in the shower. He kissed my cat goodnight then it was my turn. I commented on how perfect that night had been. He went all serious and whispered in his funny sexy eastern German dialect:

"Weiß du, mit küssen kann man sich verlieben".

(You know, one can fall in love kissing)

I giggled that falling in love is a lot more complex than that, it isn't just physical, and besides he was perfectly safe with me because we both agreed to keep to sex and refused to get into relationships

Or had he forgotten?

It would never occur to Igor to say such a dumb thing, he knows the deal and sticks to it.

As I brushed my teeth, I noticed my eyes sparkled like diamonds; they were as shiny as my cat's eyes! That also never happens with Igor.

What is best?

1. Passionate crazy raw toe curling sex with Igor, who is the perfect shag buddy in every way?

Or

2. Romantic, gentle, warm, touchy kissy expertise of Volker who turns making love into a fairy tale dream but always says something dumb afterwards?

Which one would you prefer?

Fast forward to the end of November, Volker and I had been enjoying meeting secretly for evenings of dreamlike love making for a couple of months by now. I texted to wish him happy Thanksgiving, he had no idea what Thanksgiving was but translated it as "I need you". Need him? Doesn't he mean "want to jump him"?

That night he acted a little out of character, he hadn't even shaved and took me to bed straight away. We were rolling over each other, kissing, and ahhhh the way he kisses!

The magic had kicked in and he was cupping my face with his left hand while his right arm held my waist.

He was gazing into my eyes whispering how beautiful this was: "so schön". It was perfect. I allowed myself to think this was exactly what I wanted, it couldn't get any better, and his magical kissing that was making my head spin.

At some point I gave him a terrific blow job but when he got back on top SPLASH!!! He came too soon and it landed all over my thorax, some on my right cheek, yuck, how disgusting.

He smiled that funny crooked smile of his... "Oops

sorry Schatz[1]". I wiped that unwanted white wash and saw his manhood go limp again. Sigh...

He held me close to his heart, held me so tight in his arms for so long I should have known something was wrong. Volker was caressing my back slowly; he was playing with my hair and kissing my forehead. He was purring sweet nothings in my ears; everything was as it should be.

I was in no way prepared for what was coming.

He started to get dressed and I kept teasing him playfully with pecks on his back. At some point he laid back down, my cat came up to say hello and he petted her.

"I can't do this anymore", he said

Of course I misunderstood as you would probably have too and thought I wasn't getting laid anymore tonight because of the limp situation. Then he said something that set my inner alarm off:

"I don't want to hurt you."

When people say this, it means they are going to try and hurt you within 5 minutes. His next words were: "We cannot go on like this."

"What do you mean Schatzi?" I asked, completely clueless.

"This is too much; this is not a one night stand anymore."

---

[1] *Schatz* could be translated as "darling". Literally it means "treasure"

He noticed that after ten weeks? How observant of him.

"So, this is a several night stand", I corrected, "I believe the word you are looking for is fuck buddies, sex friends, You and I are shag buddies, that's all, you are thinking way too much."

He explained that this was too much for him:

"We kiss so much and so deeply, we make love so closely, we are so intimate, you can't get enough of me and it is confusing me in here, pointing to his heart."

Now I was getting annoyed and replied as I put some robe on:

"Correction, I can't get enough of your body when it is fusing with mine, it is purely sexual. When I have sex, I really get into the moment, just like when I eat chocolate: I close my eyes and savour it. It's all about enjoying myself, that's all, nobody is falling in love here, stop worrying over nothing."

"That's just the point, he squealed, we get so high, this feels so good, don't you think it is a little weird to feel something so profound outside a loving bond?"

What was the drama queen talking about? None of this made sense.

"Come on Volker, we are having fun, I said, there is more where this is coming from, and all this without complications or strings attached, what more could you want ?"

What more could he want?

"I don't want to have fun, I want to be loved, and I want a woman for life!"

WHAT?

"Did we not agree on not wanting a relationship? Now you are complaining?"

"I don't want a relationship, he sighed, I want a soul mate."

That was too much for me: "You want a what? All I have to offer you is fabulous sex, tons of it, nothing else."

"I know, he replied, I want this kind of sex but I want it with a woman who will love me and that I will love back, that's not you, next time I feel this, I want it to mean something."

I explained that I know exactly what he is talking about for I have known this kind of love and words cannot describe how wonderful it is. Trouble is, destiny always takes it away from you in one way or another, and you are left with nothing but grief and sorrow. This kind of pain is excruciating, that's why I decided to quit love in the first place. It cuts too deep. Yet Volker wasn't satisfied with my wisdom.

"That thing we have is no longer just fucking, (*sure it is!*) we have reached a point where we either develop a relationship or we break up. I decided we should break up. Please don't cry."

I stood there with my robe wrapped around me planning what to do next, since Volker was not going to change his mind. After his departure I will have a long shower, change the sheets, feed my cat, wait... Did he expect me to cry? Hell no.

"Promise me you are not going to cry, he insisted. What am I doing?... I'm a bad person, you are better off without me."

"Sure, I yawned, if that's what you want."

Yet he tried again: "Please don't cry over me."

"Ok I won't" I answered.

Volker kissed my hand: "It's ok if you want to cry, you know."

What is it with that guy and crying?

"Dude, I purred, why should I cry? You are the one losing the perfect shag buddy that gave you fabulous sex with no string attached. On the other hand I can find another you tomorrow. Good luck finding another me..."

He told my cat he would miss her. The silly boy was breaking up with her too! On his way out he talked about being confused and perhaps needing just a break.

I stood at my window, processing what had happened and decided I was not going to let him have control of the situation. I sent him a goodbye text that was fairly clear about wanting no more contact in the future.

There! See how confused you are now, bitch!

Volker did text me at Christmas but I never replied, I do think it was arrogant of letting go of me for such a futile reason.

Next day I was discussing this with some male friends and learned this is a tactic teenage boys use to watch girls plead with them, listing reasons to stay, or to force a relationship on girls who don't want them.

31. The premonitory dream

I should have sensed this would happen, because I had had a dream about Volker a few days before.

Whenever I have dreamt of a man, it was never a good omen. The man from the dream would inevitably break up with me or try to hurt me or even con me in some ways: never a good omen indeed.

Whatever dreams I have about people often proves to be premonitory.

When I was a little girl I had this nightmare where my biological mother was slashing my tummy with a sharp razor, as I tearfully asked why, she hissed that she would make sure I would suffer whatever she would and therefore see to it that I would never achieve happiness. At the time I had no idea what she meant, but I did when said psycho tried to scare me not only physically but emotionally till I cut the cord at thirty six years old.... by filing a restraining order.

Years later I had this weird dream about looking endlessly for my girlfriend, running up large staircases and opening lots of huge windows everywhere. I desperately kept screaming her name but she would just appear and silently vanish into thin air. Years later we had a serious fight and didn't speak to each other for years. Eventually we managed to salvage our friendship and it is still going now.

Ismet, my ex boyfriend would regularly pop into my dreams too. Suddenly he was in my kitchen making some tea and smiling at how surprised I looked. My despair was immense as I'd wake and knew it was only a dream. Usually a friend would call to say she had seen Ismet somewhere.

The dream about Volker was a little freaky.

In my dream, the romantic east German marched into my apartment carrying tree bunches of flowers. Small yellow tulips, tiny red roses and multicoloured field flowers. He didn't give them to me but put them carefully on the floor, the way you would on a grave. He walked straight past me and slumbered down on my couch watching meaningless TV, totally oblivious to me. Had he even seen me? I went into the kitchen to make some hot chocolate but it was sooooo dirty. Dishes piled up all the way to the ceiling. At last I found a clean pot to warm milk in but everything was sooooo dirty and there were tea towels on the burners. Isn't this a fire hazard?

I felt extremely tired and lazy. The very thought of doing anything at all was overwhelming. I caught my reflection in the window and shivered...Was that me? Dishevelled, unshowered, wearing a stained shirt and some boring cotton knickers. How could I have opened the front door in this state? What was wrong with me? And why were those flowers on the floor? They were for me, right? Perhaps I should put them into water, Where were they? They were gone! My flowers were gone! How? When?

I began looking for them frantically till I found

them... in a closet! Who puts flowers in a closet? With no air and no sun, how were they supposed to live? It must have been Volker impersonating a couch potato while I was screaming at him that this was not how one should treat flowers!

Mew... mew... my cat woke me up. Great was my relief that this had not been real.

Why was a shag buddy making himself at home and why did I not have any control at all? That nightmare had not let me have any control over anything, not of my date, not of my appearance, not of my flowers nor of my bloody kitchen.

It had felt like I had morphed into a bored, neglected housewife. Shudders.

Yes my dreams are annoyingly premonitory.

32. My drama queen came back!

However this was not the end of my adventure with Volker... After ignoring his Christmas and Valentine texts, I melted when he suddenly just turned up at the centre in April, calling my name as I had my back turned to him, sorting out some bottles of essential oils on shelves. I turned around and saw Volker. In that instant, I could only remember the good times he had given me. Five months after walking out on me, he was missing my passionate embrace and realised he had never had it as good as with me! As I looked at him, the boyish charm, the crooked smile, the familiar laughter wrinkles and the gawky long body with the bad body posture... My resentment vanished and my desire lit up.

We talked about his work, my work, my new haircut and made lots of small talk while he undressed me with his eyes and I looked at his mouth with fond memories. I didn't even try to resist the magnet that pulled me into his arms for six delicious hours that same night. Adrenalin was rushing all over my body as I kept expecting a fight that never came. That perfect night is without the shadow of a doubt, the most romantic, passionate and sexiest night of my life. I had never felt more alive.

What was happening here? Volker stopped dating me because he thought things were too good between us, our kissing was too much, our sex was too good and he wanted to feel these things only within a relationship, right? Why then did he come back months later to give me even stronger, more intimate sex, more passion, more romance? If it was too much to handle before, how was he going to handle the really intense intimacy he was giving me now?

I avoided all serious discussions with him and decided to just enjoy what he was giving me for the time being. That fabulous night was followed by many others just as wonderful. He once asked if I had met someone else and I answered sweetly that it was none of his business. Still I could not make sense of what he really wanted from me, he used the word "we" and "us" a lot, he always paid me compliments, from my shoes to my lingerie. He kept saying everything he loved about me from my silky dark hair or my smile to the scent of my skin and the sound of my voice when I spoke French. He loved my breasts, the shape of my feet, which he loved kissing, he never tired of caressing my back or my legs, Volker just loved touching me. He seemed to love an awful lot about me, even the way I moved. My cat was pleased to see him again and he liked her too.

One night we had been making love for a couple of hours when he whispered "*je t'aime mon amour* " in my ears. I was so touched that he had learned to say this in French, but at the same time terrified of what this would mean if it were true. So I did what any responsible woman would do and... I pretended not to have heard it. He, in turn, pretended not to have said it and we pretended this was never said nor heard. Besides we all know that men don't mean it if they say this in bed.

If your man really loves you, he will repeat those words in broad daylight without any distractions. Sometimes we would have a quickie and lay in each other arms, looking at each other. He liked that better than spooning because it allowed access to my breasts and my back and at the same time he could look at me or kiss my face at will. Doesn't that sound terribly romantic to you? It did to me too.

We once had a long conversation about his home town, why he chose his profession, how he is sensitive to colours, after discovering we were both Scorpios and loved Spanish hip hop as well as soul music, he kissed my large turquoise ring and declared that people normally have this kind of conversation on their first date, before their first kiss, not after months of sleeping together.

"Do we always have to do everything backwards?" He giggled.

It was pure magic, if I hadn't known better I would have thought Volker had feelings for me. We never trusted each other enough to fully sleep together an entire night afterwards but we did fall asleep once after hours of bouncing over my bed. He was sleeping while holding my left wrist in right hand and craning my neck with his right arm. "*This is too much*, I thought, *we are getting too close and he will stub me in the back unexpectedly.*" I refused to let myself completely go and when he opened his eyes to look at me adoringly while making love again, I was almost scared of how intense we were getting. I had to look away before yelling the three dangerous words every cell in my body was screaming out, but that my brain wouldn't allow me to say. We really had a wonderful couple of months and I started to relax about the possible back stubbing.

It came one night before I left on holidays. What had I expected?

I said I wanted to see him that night before leaving for a week in Portugal the next day. Volker came, we were chatting about technologies and pollution, we had hot sex twice, we kissed endlessly, and we even had sex with our clothes on, which was a lot of fun. As I walked him to the door to kiss him goodnight, he looked at my backpack in the hall and made some joke about how many Portuguese men I would seduce that week, I pointed out this was not what that week with my friend Caroline was about. Since he insisted in this direction, I actually made an innocent joke:

"Why would I want a Portuguese when I have a Volker?"

"Mich hast du nicht", he replied. (*You don't have me*)

How cold is that?

My body was still aching from his, hematomas were forming on my inner thighs from his bony hips and my head was still spinning from the multi orgasms he kept giving me. I could still taste him while his words were now bruising my ego.

"Mich hast du nicht"

You don't have me. I didn't have him.

I had showed myself vulnerable for a brief moment and he had taken the opportunity to say something so nasty. Within seconds I had regained composure and laughed the whole thing off, we French kissed some more until he left. Once by myself I picked up my cat for some comfort. I kept pondering what he had said while she purred gently.

He was a man who gave me everything in bed, regularly, who often made innuendos about falling in love. How crazy was I to imagine for a moment that I was entitled to make one silly joke?

If that remark hurt, it could only mean that I had let Volker get too close to my heart and someone who is the boss of her sexlife cannot have that happening to her!

My next move was letting a distance between us and not having anything to do with Volker for a while. I desired him so much I almost sat on my hands not to dial his number. He must have known something was wrong because he wasn't calling either. Did he feel it too? I had no regrets for the wonderful time we had the second time around and if some day I got him out of my head... we could still be sex friends, but not while he can push my buttons.

33. How to fall out of love

The rest of the month of June was extremely busy. I had a wonderful week in Portugal with Caroline and I returned home to a ton of work, replacing some colleagues at the centre. On day time I barely had space to miss Mister "you-don't-have-me" but nights were tough. I read three books and watched countless movies to stop thinking about this situation, even put sleeping around and dating on hold as this wasn't helping. When a man is in your head he will get in the way of your enjoying sex with others, so that would be a waste of time. I prayed and meditated, talked to a good friend who was convinced I should give love another chance and stop being in denial about my East German torment. Yes I was beginning to fall in love with Volker! How did that happen? How did I not notice the alarm signals? Would he love me back? Unlikely. Would it work if I campaigned to make him love me too? It might work short term but there is still the small matter of our age difference... when he will be my age I shall be seventy years old. I doubt very much that he would still make passionate love to me then. I imagined him in different situations of my life and he didn't fit in any of those. The only place that man fit was alone with me, in our bubble. I refused to watch the situation degrade each year... No, I couldn't allow that.

However I fought against it, I kept having flashbacks of us. His face was everywhere. My dreams were filled with his hands on my hips and his lips on mine... I craved Volker's tall skinny white body like a junkie does his crack. A blog reader commented that it was normal for me to have feelings for my lover or else I would be a robot. A friend's husband explained that trust and being vulnerable to one's partner are part of a strong relationship. Maybe it works for other people but I don't want it for me.

My mind was made up; I had to unhook myself of Volker before falling irreversibly in love with him. How was I going to do this?

One morning out of the blue, I took a picture of my breasts in a lacy black bra and texted it to Volker with my caller number hidden. His reaction was immediate and here is what we texted:

V-Oh hello! What are those beautiful ladies called?

C-We are the breasts of your secret lover.

V-Mmmmmm sublime!

V-Can you show me a little more from your friends?

I sent another picture of my breasts, lace bra-less this time and added:

C-We would be pleased to feel your large hands and your sexy lips on us (and on Chantal)

V-I have friends coming over from Germany so this week is not going to be possible.

C-I will be away this weekend anyway. Was just having erotic thoughts of you, have fun.

V-You have fun too.

I felt a little embarrassed to have done this for nothing but at least I had reminded Volker that I am sexy and I have a sense of humour, perhaps he'd remember why he had liked me in the first place.

I went to work wondering if he would ever follow up and got really busy for a couple of hours. My break came up and I checked my phone. Three messages from him!

V- I would love to fuck you right now if I wasn't at work.

Yes! He still desired me!

V-Hey! How about we meet at your place at six o'clock, but I can only stay for a couple of hours.

V-Oh man! That won't work because I need to pick my mates up at nine o'clock.

Why did he feel that three hours would not be enough to shag me, get changed and pick his friends up?

V-This is how you make me feel...

And there was a picture of his gorgeous, big, shaved and much erected penis.

Yes, I had lovers send me pictures of their private parts before but this time was a complete surprise as I hadn't required one. Who knew Volker could be so kinky?

I calmly texted back

C-It's ok, I won't be home before seven pm anyway.

What do you think he answered? He who had just said six o'clock would be too late.

V-Seven o'clock your place then !!!!

Funny how men always find a way when they really want you. It can be the wrongest time, the worst place and the wrongest woman in the history of wrong women; if a man wants you, he will make sure to find the time for you. Always, always.

I had previously arranged to meet a Brazilian sexfriend at eleven that same night, so whatever would happen with Volker, I would have some distraction afterwards. If it goes well at least I won't daydream of him and if it goes wrong I would have a sexy brown shoulder to cry on.

Seven o'clock came, I was as nervous as I opened the door in little pink see-through Indian dress and pink high heels. Volker was running up the stairs and flew into my arms kissing me hard, very, very horny.

"Hot picture", he sighed.

"Yours too", I purred.

We started to feverishly undress in my hall, I dragged him by his belt all the way to my bedroom and we stumbled on my bed. The magic was back on! We never discussed his nasty pre holidays comment. In fact he probably didn't even realise what had taken place in my head.

Volker was at his best. Long languid French kisses, cupping my face, devouring my body, kissing my feet.

I had taught him to do this fabulous circle thing only black men know how to do and he gave plenty of it that night, unaware that this is a black men sexmove that drives me wild. He maintained a decent hard on the whole evening. Had he been looking at my picture all day? Hmmm. When we climaxed he fell on top of me. His heart was thumping wildly onto my chest and his bony hips still digging into my flesh. He rolled over and marvelled at me, I was sweaty and dishevelled but I never felt more alive and beautiful, reflected in my lover's adoring eyes. I kissed his fingers and closed my eyes until he fell asleep. No, I wasn't going to melt! He put an arm around me and snored ever so slightly. This was getting too sweet and I needed something to take romance out of the equation. I quietly got up and had a shower; I cuddled my cat and went back to bed wrapping my arms around a still sleepy Volker.

Was I starting to feel some tender gentle thoughts about him again? No I refused to melt!

A little kiss on the back of his neck was enough to slowly wake him up. He grabbed my left hand and turned around, revealing a sizable hard on. Yummy! I didn't listen to any words he whispered while his sexy stare was locked onto mine and our bodies fused together. At some point this felt so good that I almost screamed *I LOVE YOU*!

Instead I made some sex sounds, demanding he fucked me harder. The lovely obliging man complied and we were swept over by a whirlwind of orgasms so strong Volker was roaring like a lion when he exploded.

Post tornado, we cuddled endlessly and I marvelled at having given my body so completely without giving him my heart. Yes! I was back!

As he explained about his musician friends giving concerts in this country this summer and how they had organized their music studio, I observed him coldly, trying to spot some faults that would put me off him. Didn't find any and decided that I wasn't falling in love because there was something wrong with Volker. I wasn't falling in love because this is not the way I want to live my life.

I asked about his being late to pick his friends up but he had arranged to meet them later in the rehearsal room. When he left I didn't try to make him stay, I was my cool flirty confidant self again. As I closed the door on his goodnight kisses, I had a smile on my face and a song in my heart.

I showered again and tidied up on time for the unsuspecting Brazilian distraction to turn up.

Oswaldo is the antithesis of Volker: uncomplicated and easy going. Light years away from my East German drama queen.

The only thing these two have in common is that they are both fantastic in bed. My lower half was sore from Volker's primal amorous shagging but I really wanted to have sex again straight away with someone else to see how I would feel. I had made one big mistake with Volker; not in giving myself to him but in giving too much of myself to him. After he would leave, I would linger in bed, seeking his scent on my pillows, not showering until the morning to keep his smell on my skin, reliving every second of our intense encounters, every word and every glance, daydreaming of him, re-reading his messages. I shouldn't have done that. It had made him special, apart from others that I date. I had lost control with Volker. I needed to get control back.

The Brazilian was a gentle lover and I felt no physical discomfort. I closed my eyes and thought of the very different body that had danced into mine before and was greatly relieved when pictures of Volker wouldn't stay on my mind. He never popped up once during my steamy session nor afterwards. No thoughts of Volker at all. "*Victory!* I thought *it really works*". I normally never sleep with two men on the same day but I needed to experience this to make sure Volker was out of my system. Experience was a success! *I have fallen out of love with Volker!* Without drama, tears or severing our sexual connection. We could still be lovers but on my terms, now that I was in control of my emotions again. Yay me! I'm the boss of my sexlife again!

34. The power of words

There is a saying in English, "sticks and stones may break my bones but words will never hurt me", ever heard of it? That is not entirely true, is it? I always knew those words not to be true. Words do hurt you. Angry words, nasty words, insults, threats, those do hurt you especially because of who says them and how they say them. Words have immense power. Words can delight you, turn you on or off, comfort you or make you want to throw up. You might drop all your principles and forget about caution because of them. Whenever an old lover tries to get back into my pants after a bad breakup, he will use words to either charm me or make me feel guilty. He will use strong words that will provoke a reaction from me.

"I don't suppose you will remember me", meaning you are a slut who gets laid more than I do.

"I made such a big mistake, can you forgive me?" meaning you are a bad Christian if you don't forgive. The classic "Have you never made a mistake in your life?" is short for "Who do you think you are anyway? I'm not prepared to work too hard for you, just give in already!" Wait! I have another one for you: "You've got to give us another chance, I haven't given up on us then why have you?" All those words are designed to make us feel guilty, as if we were guilty of something. A guy makes a conscious choice to break up, which is his right. He won't hear a word we say and he walks out of our life as fast as he can. Later on, much later on, he sampled plenty other women and found that we were not so bad after all. Rather than coming back with his tails between his legs, admitting he is a bad jerk of character, oops I mean a bad *judge* of character, he either pretends to do us a favour: "You don't really want to put a stone on it, do you?" Or he tries to shift the blame on us "Why won't you give us another try? I've already said I'm sorry." Is that all? No real apology for hurting our feelings, no decent explanations of why we are better than anything else they tried after us? They make you feel as it is your fault they dropped you like a hot potato in the first place, therefore the very least we can do is to spread our legs on command. How insulting!

Why can't they just be honest and say:

"I'm not into you anymore but tonight I really desire you because you are after all a really great fuck. Tomorrow, however I will want you out of my life again, until I decide otherwise."

Yes it would sound terribly arrogant but at least it would be real and it would appeal for an honest response without guilt or pressure. It would give us a choice.

Carlos, the Portuguese alcoholic who had put me through hell during our chaotic liaison, texted me out of the blue at midnight "*Do you hate me yet?*". This triggered such a guilty reaction that I immediately texted him back "*No I don't actually hate you but...*" and it led to another round of trouble I could have done without. Another classic is when the guy makes puppy eyes at you whispering "*I don't deserve you, I know I'm not good enough for you. You need to chuck me out of your life."* Which of course has the same effect on any girl: you want to kiss the guy to comfort him. We all know how this ends don't we. The guy leaves later with his balls emptied and her feelings crushed, again. And again a few months later and again a few months after that.

Just like most of you, I have been the victim of the power of words.

I fell for that cheap trick more often than I care to remember. But I wised up and when I decided to become the boss of my sexlife, this dirty trick no longer worked with me. No matter which words were used on me. A few evenings ago I was again the recipient of the power of words again but I'm pleased to say it failed parlously. It was Valentine night and Volker, the East German kid who broke up with me so rudely three months before, really needed a great roll in the hay. Since I didn't answer his many texts favourably, he aimed carefully and texted: *"DVD?"* Sure the words triggered some good memories; our first fabulous date together, watching a DVD and ending up having romantic multiorgasms.

But I also remembered our last night. Had Volker left a door opened saying that he needed a break before seeing me again, I would have welcomed him with open arms. His decision to break up was final and without possibility of appealing. Fine, let it be final and don't come back. As I ignored Volker's text, he went for the kill and texted: *"Wanna watch a DVD with me tonight*?" Just in case I had not understood the message before. Did he push in the hope that I would get partial amnesia and say "*Come back all is forgiven*?"

Don't you just hate it when men do that?

I coldly texted "*NEIN*" and he answered "*Shade, shade, shade*", the German way to say "what a great pity".

He did want me to feel guilty. A few years ago I would have fallen for it after the first text. Now I handle things with maturity and wisdom in all things men. I identified the con in progress and made a deliberate choice not to fuel the issue by not texting back all the reasons why I want nothing to do with Volker anymore. Had I written that I didn't trust him because of this and that, Volker would have used the power of words to justify his "mistake" and the dialogue would have gone on and on until I would have surrendered. After he would have gotten what he wanted. He would then have a moment of clarity declaring this to be another mistake and needing to "find himself", which would have meant humiliation for me and just another good moment for him. Instead, the potential liar was fuming and frustrated while I rejoiced in the fact that his words had no power over me. When I did let him back into my life a few months later, I knew he would backstab me again with some words and he did when he responded to an innocent joke I made by saying "*Mich hast du nicht*" (the German for: You don't have me). I was furious that I had shown some breach in my armour and he immediately seized the opportunity to make me hurt. Some men will abuse the power of words to make you weak, all you have to do is analyse the situation coldly and refuse to let their empty words to get into your heart. Can you do that?

35. A word on lesbian love

We cannot talk extensively about sexual freedom without mentioning lesbian love.

I'm not talking about going down on some girl during a threesome to make your man happy, I'm talking about dating a girl you really like and letting desire take over without fear or guilt.

Pleasure can come in many shapes and it would be a shame to miss out on a moment of happiness just because the person offering it is not conform to everyone's standards. I have had some unforgettable orgasms and wonderful times with some ladies over the years and it didn't make me a lesbian, I still date men.

There is nothing to be afraid of. Not to mention the advantage of not needing birth control, the lack of premature ejaculators and hardly any STD's risks.

Valerie, a beautiful porn actress in Milan rocked my world and my body for a summer. Trudie a cute chiropractician, Desdemona a firy bresilian dancer in Geneva and Deirdre a tough business woman in Paris really made me question my commitment to singlehood and I almost fell in love with Shakira, the best looking Singaporian transexual acrobat from a famous travelling circus. We used to french kiss in public totally oblivious to raised eyebrows around us. They were all women who loved women and had loved me for a few nights of my life. They were each special and enthralling, captivating, compelling and irresistible. I never lied about being attracted to men and have no regrets about our getting together in the past. Should I meet again another woman who would be as smart, funny, caring, warm and creative as my lesbian lovers had been, I would not rule out giving into her. If she would accept my way of life, that is.

So if you know a special woman who is very much into you, don't be afraid to like her back. It doesn't mean you will never want men again. And if it happens... then you have been blessed with trough love and it will be worth trying.

36. Valentine's alone, so what?

Many people, men and women, feel inadequate and embarrassed if they don't have a partner on Valentine day. Especially with the huge amount of advertisement it generates, red hearts are popping up everywhere along with red roses and chocolates. Shame on you if you don't have a lover who spends money on you at Valentine. How silly!

I am always single, all year and that includes Valentine day, too. To smug married women who show off a card or a rose, I will gladly answer that my lovers often bring me presents during the year, chocolates, perfume, flowers, sexy lingerie and scented candles. And to the ones who make sure the entire office knows they are planning to get laid that night, I will giggle that I get laid more often that they do and not out of obligation because one has to shag the missus on that day. Hooray for the couples who genuinely have Valentine fun, Boo hoo to those who use it to make lonely women feel even emptier.

People have the annoying tendency to confuse alone with lonely. One does not automatically imply the other. How many married women feel terribly lonely in their relationships because their men treat them as if they were invisible? Many. You could be at a crowded party with your boyfriend and still be very alone. Being part of a couple does not guaranty happiness, emotional support or companionship. It can be the case but there is no guaranty. So what did

I do this Valentine 2011? I had a great time. I sent Valentine messages to all my real friends, men and women. I cooked myself a tasty meal, got into comfy pyjamas and watched soapy romantic comedies all evening with my lovely cat who kept purring from the simple joy of spending a quiet evening at home with mummy all to herself. The phone had ringed several times during the day and texts kept appearing on my screen. Past lovers, current ones, lovers who had broken up a few months before, others who are hoping to date me soon. Karim, Volker and Mark were especially persistent. I wouldn't pick up and yet they each kept texting very sexy powerful words to break my resistance. But I felt so good at home, warm and safe, loved up with my cat, laughing at those really funny movies, my tummy full with great food and a cup of hot chocolate coming up. I felt anything but lonely, I felt safe, wanted and in control of my life. I answered an email from Igor to accept a date on the next day, looking very much forward to a post Valentine shag, I blogged and updated my Facebook until I fell asleep with my cat in my arms who challenged my Olympic gold medal in snoring most of the night. There! I had a fabulous time without a partner. So can you. Of course your circumstances might be different, you might not like romantic comedies and you might not have a cat or some friends. But even so, there is no need to be depressed. Treat yourself. Go on a date or don't go on a date but treat yourself anyway.

Be nice to yourself. Money is short? Then do something nice for yourself that won't cost anything. A long bubble bath with candles all around, a long shower, paint your toenails, make your favourite drink or cook yourself a little feast – yes for you alone. Read that great book you never have time to. Do something for yourself; you can love yourself even if you think no one else does. If you love yourself, it will show in your body language and it will attract positive actions from others. Be your first number one fan.

37. It is better to be single because...

Out of all the women I interviewed for this book and all the girlfriends I spoke to, 80 % are not happy within their marriage or relationship. They each had to abandon a large part of who they are and their men didn't.

I want to let you in on a little secret that many of us can't even imagine: it is best to be single than married!

I am so bored with smug freshly married women who look at their single girlfriends with arrogance and declare condescendingly: *Aawww don't worry, you will eventually find someone too.* Say what????

Or the classical: *what about you? Still alone?* I'm not alone, I am free, unlike you.

Fast forward a few years later when said smug married woman is tired of multitasking job, marriage and kids, barely gets any sex or consideration, struggles for money to feed everybody, needs to budget carefully with hubby's approval, never gets any time for herself and sometimes get cheated on with single women. The single women she was despising since she has been a man's official half.

Who is worried now? Not the single woman who "*is still alone and will eventually find somebody*". That girl is still getting lots of great sex with handsome strangers, still financially independent and master of her own destiny, not slowed down or submitted to her man's control.

My friend Michelle once told me being married and being loved is not the same thing at all. How right.

If I wanted to really find someone long term it would be done, but I'm enjoying my life so much I'm not prepared to be slowed down by marriage and its many obligations, never again. Please don't get me wrong, I'm not saying nobody should get married, after all I have done it twice myself. I'm saying, if you find a fantastic man and marry him, fine, do marry him, but don't turn your nose up in a superior attitude because you never know what will happen in a few years. Men have a nasty habit of abandoning ship when things go wrong, your girlfriends, single or not, will still be there years later, offering support and comfort.

Why do I feel it is best to be single on many levels? Let's start at the beginning.

Work wise, it is best to be single as you decide on your schedules yourself and make decisions that are best for you without considering your man. Can you work later today? Can you attend that seminar out of town next weekend? Can you replace your boss? Can you take a further course to be promoted? Can you be at that business function or work lunch? Can you swap a shift with a colleague? All of this is for you and you alone to decide, when you are single. You get to decide.

Socially, it is best to be single. You can plan your time for hobbies, activities and sport outside work.

If you get asked out, you can change your planning within seconds without making sure no one will be offended or no one forcing you to put his agenda before yours. What about likes that are forced on women by their men? Sarah laments that she loves opera and really misses it because her husband won't go. "Sarah why don't you just go to the opera by yourself? I love ballet, my second husband hated it and I always went to "Giselle" or "the swan lake" alone either he liked it or not."

Christina complains that she has to cook greasy fat steaks daily because her husband loves them and refuses to eat healthy, making her put on weight in the process. *"Christina, you could either educate your husband about the consequences of eating unhealthy/ take up sport to lose some fat/ cook it just for him and do another dish for you while he gorges on fats."* When you are the sole master on board, you are free to do as you please.

Friends and relatives are welcome in your house without you having to ask permission first. Last minute weekends or breaks with friends coming up? You can just take off spontaneously anywhere anytime without feeling guilty or scared of consequences. Do you feel like getting up at 2am for a salmon sandwich and an action movie? How about a nice long shower just for the sake of it? Or surfing all night chatting with cyber friends when you can't sleep? All these perks are within your reach when you live by yourself. If there is a guy snoring in your bed, chances are he will get up, disturb whatever you were enjoying for yourself and order you back to bed *because it is 2 am* !

Once you obey and get back to bed against your will, he probably won't even have the sense to thank you with a nice quickie for your company.

Financially, it is best to be single as you are solely in charge of your earnings and spending. Of course if you are a mother you do have sacrifices to make as your children's financial needs to be placed before yours. This is never easy but can be done joyfully with a little faith and lots of love. No man to control your spending or forbid you to buy something he doesn't approve of. No man to drink your hard earned salary before you have time to pay the rent, school tuitions and buy groceries.

Safety wise it is better to be single. No brutalities from a violent man who confuses wife with punch bag.

Last but not least, it makes more sense sexually to be single.

When you officially belong to your man, he no longer appreciates you. Desire flies out of the window when he takes you for granted every day. Besides how could he feel turned on by his servant-cook-cleaning lady-clothes washer-co decorator-co bill payer?

How does a man get ready for a date?

He will shave and shower carefully, wash and condition his hair, do a few push ups for his tummy to look fit and he will eat some sweets to have a nice fresh breath if his date is a non smoker. He will sometimes even put on sexy underpants and work on his looks, bad boy, casual or romantic. During the date he will be charming, funny and interesting. He will give her the hottest sex he can, to make sure she finds him better than all her previous experiences.

He wants to make an impression.

What does a man do before going to bed with his wife or go home to his partner?

Nothing.

He knows she is his, no more conquering required, He doesn't care about making an impression.

End of story.

The more serious a relationship gets the less sexy and romantic it becomes with courtesy and good manners going out of the window. Even you won't feel like making an effort unless a special occasion calls for it.

The sexlife of a single woman who is the boss of her sexlife is much more interesting and orgasmic than the life of most married women. It is as every date is a very first date even if it is the same guy again and again.

I'm not saying having your own man is wrong or annoying, I'm just letting you know a great sexlife is hardly ever on the menu of a couple, there are always more important things to do like educating your children or paying bills.

38. Conclusion

Sisters, it is time to be in charge of your love live and your sex life. If you want no more love pain nor heartbreaks. If you are tired of crying after being let down again and again. You need to fight men with their own weapon... a liberated sexlife without emotional involvement.

Even if you reclaim your heart and become the boss of your sexlife, you might have relapses but there is nothing to worry about, those moments of weakness are perfectly dealable.

I have such moments of doubts myself when every now and then I meet a man who is so amazing, so patient, hard working and considerate, not to mention an exceptional lay. The kind of man who has the same hobbies and centre of interest as I do, shares my love of cats, my tastes in food and music. He is so irresistible when we cuddle and spoon after coming together and he avoids the topics that upset me. Should I not let my heart melt when I watch him sleep while he is still holding my hand? Dare I listen to his intimate voice whispering that he loves me or am I right to pretend not to hear it? Is it reasonable to stare back into his adoring eyes when we are making love so intensely? Are we connecting too deeply? Would he kiss me post sex for hours if he wasn't that much into me? When is he going to backstab me? This cannot be real; did I kiss my fair share of toads and now found a prince? Does it mean something that he has kissed every inch of my body in a non sexual way too? Why are we so compatible if we couldn't be together? Can I afford the luxury of giving that one a chance? Maybe just one more time? Just this once? Just this man?

Must I always be so bossy, so scared of love, scared of losing control and getting hurt again? What shall I do? What shall I do? Questions keep pouring out over my head.

Temptations! Temptations!

I'm not perfect, I know temptation too, but then my brain kicks in and I remember that today's prince charming could be turn into tomorrow's domestic tyrant if given half a chance.

I imagine my mister perfect unshaved and angry arguing with me over who takes out the trash, who pays which bill and when the in laws are visiting again. And I feel better already. Those little relapses happen to me too but sense of survival takes over. There is almost always some kind of expiry date on any relationship or connection so we might as well quit while we are ahead.

Ladies, if I can do this, so can you. Become the boss of your sexlife today and discover the power of freedom.

Discover it today!

THE END...

...of my book, but...

THE BEGINNING OF YOUR NEW LIFE

www.ingramcontent.com/pod-product-compliance
Lightning Source LLC
Chambersburg PA
CBHW060251290526
45789CB00001B/288